To my good
friend Raquel,

You are Amazing.

Thank you!

DIVERSIFY OR DIE

Diversity. Inclusion. Evolution. Success.

DIVERSIFY OR DIE

Diversity. Inclusion. Evolution. Success.

By Eric L. Guthrie, Esq. CDE

© 2016 by Eric Guthrie. All rights reserved.

Published by Better ME Better WE Publishing, Arlington, VA

No part of this publication can be reproduced, stored in a retrieval system, or transmitted in any form by any means, electronic, mechanical, photocopying, recording, scanning, or other wise, without the prior written permission of the author or publisher, except in the case of brief quotations embodied in critical reviews and certain other noncommercial uses permitted by copyright law. Requests to the publisher should be addressed to Better ME Better WE Publishing, PO Box 9850, Arlington, VA 22219, USA, 1-202 709 9219, or online at www.BetterMEBetterWE.com.

Limited Liability/Disclaimer of Warranty: While the publisher, editor, and author have used their best efforts in preparing this book, they make no representations or warranties with respect to the accuracy or completeness of the contents of this book, or the websites referenced therein, and specifically disclaim any implied warranties of merchantability or fitness for a particular purpose. No warranty may be created or extended by diversity professionals or diversity materials. The advice and strategies herein may not be suitable for your situation. You should directly consult with the author or a diversity professional before implementing diversity plans, policies, or other diversity efforts.
Neither the publisher nor author shall be liable for any loss of profit or other commercial damages, including but not limited to: special, incidental, consequential, or other damages. The author and publisher, individually or corporately, do not accept any responsibility for any liabilities resulting from the actions of any parties involved.

Bulk purchases of this book for educational training purposes or corporate distribution are available. For orders and general information of our other products and services, please contact our Customer Care Department at Better ME Better WE, PO Box 9850, Arlington, VA 22219, USA, 1-202 709 9219, or online at www.BetterMEBetterWE.com.

Cover and interior design by Brian D. Johnson,
Creative Design Consultant at Doran Designs, LLC
Editing by Tanya Brockett, MBA

ISBN: 978-0-9979332-0-8 (Hardcover)
ISBN: 978-0-9979332-1-5 (Paperback)

Printed in the United States of America.

CONTENTS

ACKNOWLEDGMENTS	i
CHAPTER 1 – Diversify or Die	**1**
The Interplay Between Power and Diversity	2
Diversity Lessons are Everywhere, You Just Have to Look	3
Why Should I Care About Diversity and Inclusion?	5
Diversity and Inclusion Challenges	5
The Challenge of the Diversity Department	9
An Example of the Use of Time, Money and Effective Resources	10
How Can Diversity Help My Business Make Money?	11
CHAPTER 2 – Delving into Darwinism and Diversity	**12**
The Theory of Evolution in the Business Environment	13
Darwin's Sense for Adventure	14
Darwin's Open and Curious Mind	15
Survival of the Fittest	16
Natural Selection	16
Revisiting Darwin in the Business Context	17
More Businesses are Created that can Possibly Survive	17
Traits Vary Among Organizations, Leading to Different Rates of Survival and Organizational Growth	19
Trait Differences are Heritable by Successive Management Chains	21
The Inhibitors of Evolution	22
CHAPTER 3 – The Diversity Equation and Definition of Diversity	**24**
Definitions of Diversity?	25
The Evolution of a Definition	30
Responsible Sale of Goods and Services	30
The Definition of Diversity for Not for Profits	35
The Definition of Diversity for Small Businesses	36
The Definition of Diversity and Inclusion for Government Agencies	37

CHAPTER 4 – A Modern Socio-Economic History of Diversity	41
Evolutionary Diversity Timeline Methodology	42
Evolutionary Diversity Timeline	43
Evolutionary Diversity Timeline Analysis	49
The Economic Leverage of the Multicultural Economy	50
Workforce 2000	52
Workforce 2020	52
Mergers and Acquisitions in the Diversity Timeline	53
Social Media	54
Diversifying Social Media	55
CHAPTER 5 – The Evolution of Diversity and Inclusion Beyond Affirmative Action	59
Diversity and Inclusion Should Not Replace Affirmative Action	61
Who are the Enemies of Evolution in Your Organization?	62
Mid Level Management Behavior Example #1	64
Mid Level Management Behavior Example #2	64
How Can You Tell When Diversity Efforts are Working?	65
The Anatomy of a Diversity Department	65
CHAPTER 6 – The Diversity Department	69
The Definition of Diversity and Inclusion and the Diversity Department	69
Where is Your Diversity Department Located in your Organization?	71
Common and Costly Diversity Mistakes	73
What is the Status of Diversity in your Company?	74
The Critical Diversity Component: Middle Management	76
Diversity Training for Middle Managers	76
The Evolution of Diversity Training	78
Diversity Training Follow Up	79
Diversity Policies	80
Evolution is not Immediate	81
"Diversity of Thought"	81
CHAPTER 7 – Powerful Tools for Evolution: The Employee Resource Committees and Diversity Councils	83
ERC Lessons Learned	

Is Your ERC a Group that Meets to Complain About Management?	84
Diversity Sales and Marketing Measurement #1 – Understand your Cultural Audience	88
Diversity Sales and Marketing Measurement #2 – Diversity within Race and Culture	88
Diversity Sales and Marketing Measurement #3 – The Diversity Cost - Benefit Analysis	88
Diversity Sales and Marketing Measurement #4 – Closing Conversion	89
Diversity Councils	89
Diversity Council Leadership	90
Support from Organizational Leadership	91
Focus on Long Term Business Goals	91
Selection of Members for the Diversity Council	92
Evolution of Employee Resource Groups and Diversity Councils	92
CHAPTER 8 – Diversity Metrics and Measurement of Evolution	**94**
You Cannot Manage Diversity Unless You Measure Diversity	94
The Time Factor in Diversity Metrics and Measurement	100
Time Factor	100
The Future is Now	101
CHAPTER 9 – The Connection to Diversity and the Stock Market	**102**
Artificial Interference with Evolution	**103**
The Analysis of Diversity and the Stock Market	**104**
The Diversify or Die Stock Analysis	**105**
DiversityInc.	**106**
Public v. Privately Owned Companies	**107**
Overall Stock Analysis Summary	**131**
CHAPTER 10 – Words of Motivation for Evolution	**134**
Words to Motivate Management Actions	134
Progressive Motivational Quotes	135
Use Your Definition of Diversity to Motivate Your Employees	148

CHAPTER 11 – Diversify and Thrive	**150**
Why Should I Care About Diversity and Inclusion	150
Good News	150
Afterword	154
Bibliography	156
Index	171

ACKNOWLEDGEMENTS

After writing this book, I realized it takes a team to write a book, and a good team to write a good book. Although the author puts his initial thoughts on paper, or a computer, it takes a talented team to transition those thoughts from initial writings to a published book. I was fortunate to have a good team.

Thank you to Randy Peyser, Author One Stop. I first talked to Randy about this book in 2011. For five years I would reach out to Randy every now and then to give an update or ask a question. Randy always had time for me, and an answer that would move my work forward. Finally, in 2016, I officially used Randy's services to help publish Diversify or Die.

Thank you to Tanya Brockett. As an editor, Tanya continually made my book better every time. Tanya's ability to grasp the grand concept of my book and exhibit attention to detail was the combination my book needed to be ready for publication.

Thank you to Tony Termini for his contribution to Chapter 9 of the book. Tony's ability to research, review, coordinate, and communicate financial data was a huge benefit to
the chapter.

Thank you to my sisters Tracey Guthrie MD and Kate Guthrie PhD for being excellent sounding boards and a wonderful source of support for this book and in life.

Finally, thank you to Robert C. Webber III and Alonzo M. Robertson, Esq. for their friendship, guidance, and support. Both are true friends and Morehouse Brothers.

CHAPTER 1
DIVERSIFY OR DIE

"Extinction follows chiefly from the competition of tribe with tribe."

— Charles Darwin, *The Descent of Man*

Diversify or Die

Diversify or die sounds dramatic, doesn't it? How does the failure to implement diversity and inclusion in your organization result in extinction? The answer is in the key word—competition—in Charles Darwin's quote above. Competition, the struggle for resources, natural or engineered, is the key component where constant failure may lead to extinction. In comparing evolution and business, if "extinction follows chiefly from the competition of tribe with tribe," it follows in the business world that extinction follows chiefly from the competition of business with business.

Of course, business competition is not a new concept. Every business owner uses available resources to start a business to compete in the market. Business success comes at the expense of other businesses with one or more of the following inferior resources: employees, leadership, products, infrastructure, marketing, sales, market share, technology, or financing. Failure in any one of these categories gives the stronger business a competitive advantage, causing the weaker business to evolve or face the end of business life: extinction.

DIVERSIFY OR DIE: DIVERSITY. INCLUSION. EVOLUTION. SUCCESS.

"Diversify or die" is most likely a worse case scenario, but it is possible. For example, the extinction of former technology giant Nokia was attributed, in part, to the lack of diversity in Nokia leadership. In May 2013, Fortune Magazine published an article entitled "Why Corporate Giants Fail to Change." In the article, Julian Birkinshaw, Professor of Strategic and International Management at London Business School, used Nokia as an example of a failed corporate giant. Mr. Birkinshaw gave five reasons for Nokia's failure and the fourth reason was the lack of diversity.

In addressing the lack of diversity, the article stated:

> *Nokia's top executives were all Fins of similar age and background, and this surely hampered their ability to make sense of their changing business environment. Of course, we are all more comfortable working with people with similar worldviews and as a result we end up with inevitable blind spots. The solution? Hire people with different frames of reference from our own, or at least find a way to bring their point of view to the table. In the late 1990s, Infosys (INFY) had a program called "Voice of Youth" designed to bring the insights of the under-30 crowd to the attention of the 50-something executive team.*

The other reasons for Nokia's failure included "ossified" management processes, old and narrow metrics, a disenfranchised front line, and intolerance of failure. Nokia—once a clear leader in cell phone technology—failed to diversify, and as a result, they failed to evolve and ultimately, faced extinction.

Recognizing the signs of extinction is not always easy. I am sure the leaders of Nokia were very comfortable in their daily business surroundings, but that comfort was in part due to a failure to engage in a diversity journey on an employee, leadership, and organizational level. But I argue these five reasons have one thing in common: Keeping power in the same place with the same people.

The Interplay Between Power and Diversity

Diversity and inclusion actions in an organization can mean a basic shift in power at some level. There are many reasons for an organization to engage in diversity, but each reason has the potential to shift power. Recognizing the relationship between power and diversity led to long and in-depth conversations about diversity with many executives.

Most of the conversations with executives revealed that they believed in diversity and felt it should be embraced; the problem was they rarely felt diversity actions were necessary. In other words, the concept of diversity is great, but just leave it as a concept, action is not required. These executives did not believe in diversity and inclusion actions because many felt it took power away from their decision-making process, which included the power to:

- Hire
- Assign work
- Pay salaries, bonuses, or stock options
- Write performance reviews
- Promote
- Terminate

Although, many managers and executives viewed diversity and inclusion as a policy that may take their power, they were faced with a political reality. Diversity was gaining traction and companies were embracing diversity in the face of a changing business environment. The short-term solution for many executives was to publicly accept diversity and create "business reasons" when they felt diverse practices should not be used.

Diversity Lessons are Everywhere, You Just Have to Look
In one of my diversity positions, I was assigned to review a diversity training session and provide feedback about the quality of the training. As I had prior experience in diversity and diversity training, I was prepared for the same type of diversity training discussions related to race and gender.

On the first day of the multiday diversity training, we participated in an exercise that compared the world of right-handed people to that of left-handed people. After the exercise was over, we talked about the results. As a right-handed person, I was surprised to learn some of the challenges of the left-handed participants. As a right-handed person, I exist in the "right-handed world" and never give a second thought to what it is like to exist in a "left-handed world." But within thirty minutes, I was starting to understand the challenges of a left-handed person. Then it occurred to me that the lack of understanding I had for left-handed people may be the same lack of understanding a person from one culture or race has for another culture or race. A powerful lesson.

The right/left-handed exercise was a "gateway exercise." The exercise provided a safe way to gain a new perspective and understanding, and realize there are many more perspectives than one's own. The question in my mind was, did everyone else make the connection?

As I continued to review the diversity training, I paid close attention to the impact this exercise had on individual participants. As with many diversity trainings, some understood the value of the exercise and some did not. Since this was the gateway exercise, I held out hope there would be many other lessons to show the value of diversity and inclusion. These lessons of diversity would not only come from the trainers, but from the participants as well.

In the same diversity training later in the week, we took part in an exercise where we were given chips that had different colors and value. The goal of the exercise was to follow the rules to bargain and exchange chips with other participants to increase the value of our own chips. When the exercise started, everyone was bargaining with each other, trying to make deals to obtain higher value chips and win the competition. However, something interesting happened midway through the exercise. I noticed a white male executive sitting on the floor with his legs stretched out and crossed, and his back against the wall. Near the end of the exercise, I sat down next to him and I asked him, "Why are you sitting here? Are you not interested in this exercise?"

He said, "Absolutely. I had one very valuable chip and the rest were worthless. I gave the valuable chip to one of the guys and told him, 'I am giving you this chip and when you succeed because I gave you the chip, you have to take care of me."

I was astounded. This approach never occurred to me or anyone else in the training for that matter. Again, diversity lessons are everywhere; you just have to look.

The beauty of his unique approach was the instructions to the exercise did not prevent the donation of a chip to another training participant. This executive found a way to think "out of the box," follow the rules, and have his chip work for him even though he gave it away. This was another important lesson in diversity for me—the relationship between power and diversity.

Why Should I Care about Diversity and Inclusion?

Human beings are emotional creatures, so most decisions are emotionally based. There are essentially two reasons we buy something: to receive pleasure or to avoid pain.

In the business world, receiving pleasure also means: increased sales, profits, or bottom line; better employee morale; increased innovation; and higher productivity. Avoiding pain also means less employee problems, less unnecessary lawsuits, and not losing competitive advantage. The diversity and inclusion pleasure and pain incentives sound wonderful in principle, but they are not easy to obtain.

Diversity and Inclusion Challenges

At times, the greatest challenge is to accept the challenge in the first place. Once the challenge is accepted, the resolution is one step closer.

Diversity and inclusion has many challenges. In order to apply diversity, the relevant fundamental challenges must be addressed. It is important to note that none of these challenges are short-term challenges with easy solutions. These challenges are:

1. Lack of agreement regarding the definition of diversity.
2. Failure to connect diversity to the mission statement and objectives of the organization.
3. Failure to directly connect diversity to return on investment.
4. Challenges in implementing diversity policies and programs.
5. Failure to act, e.g., always giving the employees surveys to see what the employees think, but then not doing anything.

DIVERSIFY OR DIE: DIVERSITY. INCLUSION. EVOLUTION. SUCCESS.

6. Employee and manager challenges to the change in corporate culture, e.g., "we have always done things this way."
7. Failure to develop diversity metrics.
8. Failure to adequately fund diversity programs.
9. Failure to completely or adequately use the diverse employees in marketing efforts and social media.
10. Using diversity training that does not work.
11. Failure to use employee resource groups and diversity councils to their full potential.

This is an impressive list of challenges. Why should an organization care about any one of these challenges and failures? Stating that diversity is "the right thing to do" is noble and correct, but the bottom line is the bottom line. The stronger the connection that diversity has to the bottom line, the stronger the case for diversity—and when used correctly—the stronger the return on investment. The reasons why an organization should care about diversity include:

1. Lack of executive consensus on diversity leads to ineffective diversity efforts where organizational time and resources are spent facing unnecessary challenges on multiple fronts.
2. Statistics clearly show that the ethnic and cultural diversity in the United States has been steadily increasing, which impacts US organizations in the following manner:
   a. Substantial increase in a diverse customer base.
   b. Substantial increase in diverse employment pool.
   c. Substantial increase of the purchasing power of the ethnic diversity community.
3. Organizations that have inadequate diversity presence in their employee population or marketing communications may face public relations backlash.
4. Engaging in effective diversity efforts improves the following:
   a. Employee morale
   b. Quality of hires
   c. Rate of retention
   d. Rate and quality of innovation
   e. Organizational creativity

The diversity and inclusion challenges are different based on the organizational level. The solutions to the challenges are more elusive, especially when all levels of the organization are not communicating in an honest, solution-oriented manner.

As this book presents a very balanced and structured argument; it will also address the perceived negative opinions of diversity and inclusion. Some of the negative opinions about diversity and inclusion include:
1. Diversity is a divisive issue that may create unnecessary tension in an organization
2. Diversity is essentially a new quota system
3. Diversity candidates are "not qualified"

The acknowledgement of these negative opinions is important as they are commonly used to discredit or prevent the use of diversity and inclusion programs. These opinions are poor excuses compared to the overwhelming amount of data substantiating the US demographic shift and the increased spending power of the ethnic diversity community. The responses to these negative opinions are easy:

1. Many companies have successfully included diversity into their corporate culture without conflict or disagreements.
2. When the "quota" conversation is raised, many people defend the quota system as an older version of affirmative action. My usual response is that diversity IS a quota system. Use diversity to broaden your sales and marketing and watch your sales, productivity, and market share quotas increase.
3. Any manager who makes a decision about an applicant's qualifications before looking at their education and credentials and comparing them to the applicant pool is clearly discriminating in the employment decision. The organization should remove this manager from management.

The common list of diversity challenges based on level include:

Typical Employee-Level Diversity Challenges
- Lack of diverse managerial and executive role models
- Employees' qualifications are questioned by managers and peers
- Lower rate of promotions and pay increases
- Frustration by executive failure to recognize individual and organizational diversity issues
- Frustration by organizational failure to communicate diversity initiatives and failure to achieve published diversity goals

Typical Management-Level Diversity Challenges
- Do not believe that diversity impacts the bottom line
- View diversity as a policy or practice that takes over their ability to make managerial decisions
- Cannot distinguish between affirmative action, EEO, and diversity
- View diversity efforts as a challenge to their status in the organization including, but not limited to any one of the following: white, male, English speaker, baby boomer, heterosexual, non-veteran, or non-disabled
- Have little access to quality diversity training that includes connections to the bottom line of the organization

Typical Executive-Level Diversity Challenges
- Lack of vision and leadership to create comprehensive diversity policies and practices
- Challenges in creating an inclusive environment for diverse employees
- Challenges in keeping midlevel managers accountable to diversity goals
- Pressure from employees to address diversity issues
- Lack of funding for diversity efforts
- Unsure how to incorporate diversity into the organization and business model

These challenges often fall under the jurisdiction of the diversity department.

The Challenge of the Diversity Department

Executives often look to the diversity department to resolve issues and create an inclusive workplace. Diversity and inclusion departments are usually compliance or human resources employees or attorneys, especially labor and employment attorneys. The ability of the diversity department to lead meaningful organizational change is limited in the absence of formal diversity education or training, and when there is a lack of funding or resources.

Historically, diversity is commonly linked to affirmative action and equal employment opportunity (EEO). From that perspective, diversity has been viewed as a legally mandated program whose only purpose is to comply with the regulations related to affirmative action or EEO. Someone who is "anti-diversity" would argue the failure of a company to use diversity to hire, retain, promote, market, and sell to people of color, different cultures, women, disabled, LGBT, or various ages is in no way related to the success or failure of the company.

Despite the evolution of diversity, the concept of diversity is controversial and opponents of diversity use the historical similarities with affirmative action and equal employment opportunity to limit, marginalize, and contest the very ideals and benefits of diversity. I understand the continued perpetuation of this viewpoint, as many organizations have combined diversity, EEO, and affirmative action into one department or even one position. Indeed, I have served in those "hybrid diversity positions" myself.

When I served in hybrid diversity positions, I found them to be severely limiting and shortsighted. The company's executive focus related to diversity, when the company had an executive focus related to diversity, was on the legalities of affirmative action and EEO and mitigating the risks of their actions or inactions. Diversity was part of the job description with affirmative action and EEO, but not used in a substantive way to add value to the company's bottom line.

I usually recommended different ways to use diversity programs and diversity training to lower costs by increasing recruiting efforts, employee retention, and employee engagement. Although I longed to use deeper diversity efforts, I did not have the authority or the resources to uncouple my diversity responsibilities from affirmative action and EEO.

An Example of the Use of Time, Money, and Effective Resources

In one diversity leadership position, my department was placed in a situation where the executives wanted to deeply reduce sponsorship levels in diversity MBA and engineering organizations. Our company was not receiving the number of applicants and hires to justify the cost of sponsorship. Our company was sending human resources recruiters to diversity recruiting conferences. The human resources recruiters talked to applicants and brought the résumés back to the corporate office. The recruiters marketed the interested candidates to hiring managers. As this approach did not result in enough hires, the return on investment did not justify the cost. I decided to evolve the diversity recruiting approach.

As sponsors, we had online access to student résumés prior to the recruiting conference, so I convened a team of hiring managers to review them in advance. The managers were always consistently amazed by the quality of résumés in the system. After the hiring managers reviewed the résumés, we contacted the students that met the position qualifications before the conference to see if they had any interest in interviewing with our company. I also reduced the number of human resources employees and greatly increased the number of hiring managers attending the recruiting conference.

This approach allowed the hiring manager to conduct interviews at the conference. This booked our interview schedule at the conference over capacity and enabled us to conduct first interviews, and sometimes second interviews, on the spot. Prior to using this strategy, our interview booths were usually empty. The first conference where we implemented this strategy, our interview booths were booked solid and we had to use any space we could find to conduct interviews. On occasion, the hiring manager even made an offer on the spot.

As the numbers from this approach greatly increased our interviews, offers, and acceptances from these diversity conferences, this approach also reduced costs, as the company had a streamlined interview process.

Managers did not have to spend as much money flying in applicants and booking hotel rooms. This proved my business case, and our sponsorship levels remained unchanged during my tenure.

How Can Diversity Help My Business Make Money?

I left these hybrid diversity positions, continued my analysis of diversity, and engaged in diversity training and consulting. That freedom allowed me to make the case to executives that diversity is much more than affirmative action and EEO. With greater freedom came greater abilities to present diversity as a business imperative rather than a component in the position description with affirmative action and EEO. The usual response, especially with small businesses, is, "how can diversity help my business make more money?" This is a fair question.

The usual course of action is to review an organization's business plan and marketing plan to determine if they are marketing and selling to the diversity community. Then we discuss the ways they can sell to and service the diversity community, and diversity suddenly becomes a business opportunity.

Next we discuss the ability of their current staff to sell, service, and provide customer support to the diversity community. This approach includes reviewing the demographics of their customer base and the demographics of their employee base. This analysis of the application of diversity led me to also analyze well beyond legal, affirmative action, EEO, human resources, recruiting, and retention. In order to truly consult and train on diversity, I found I was required to analyze business practices, marketing, sales, global efforts, cross cultural communications/collaborations, and stock market performance. The combination of all the skills in my diversity toolbox were absolutely necessary to write this book.

CHAPTER 2
DELVING INTO DARWINISM AND DIVERSITY

"[The] preservation of favourable individual differences and variations, and the destruction of those which are injurious, I have called Natural Selection or Survival of the Fittest."

— Charles Darwin *On The Origin of Species*

This is the most commonly known, and misquoted, statement from On The Origin of Species. I am sure Charles Darwin did not have any idea of the magnitude these words would have on the world for over a century. What does this quote really mean?

Wildlife nature shows record a lioness or cheetah chasing a gazelle or wildebeest, and at the end of the successful chase the narrator says, "the big cat has obtained her prey and her pride will eat tonight. This is survival of the fittest." Nature shows are full of comments like these. This commentary has even made its way to pop culture and the business world when the bigger person or the bigger company exerts their size and power over the smaller person or company. But that is not what Darwin is saying.

Darwin does not mention the larger creatures hunting or killing smaller creatures in this context in On *The Origin of Species*. In order to fully understand Darwin's statement, one has to look at the critical clause in the quote: "favourable individual differences and variations." Using this lens, we realize, the lion will always be stronger than the wildebeest or the cheetah faster than the gazelle, so stating the obvious does not represent the intent of the statement. However, a weaker lion that does not have "favourable individual differences and variations" may not survive in the pride because it cannot hunt as well or defend itself in a fight against another lion. In addition, a male lion may not be given the chance to procreate because he cannot win mating contests against competing male lions. If the weaker lions cannot procreate, their unfavorable genetic line will eventually cease to exist. A stronger lion pride is the result of the extinction of the weaker genes.

Fortunately for humans, another factor in determining survival is intelligence. When surrounded by animals that were stronger, faster, venomous, and more ferocious, humans used intelligence to adapt to their environment. Intelligence is one of the *"favourable individual differences and variations"* that humans use to survive. As humans are helpless at birth and totally dependent on adult humans for survival, intelligence is a learned variation. It is not until the human has fully learned their *"favourable individual differences and variations"* that they can use intelligence to their advantage.

The final factor worthy of note is adaptation to the environment. Even though man is arguably the most intelligent, it does not mean they cannot be destroyed. Even the smallest forms of life—viruses and bacteria—which do not have any intelligence, have the capacity to infiltrate, adapt, and cause major damage inside the human body. Viruses have even adapted to antibiotics that were destroying them for decades. In this scenario, evolution did not take thousands of years; viruses evolved in decades. In short, the faster a species evolves, the faster they can ensure survival.

The Theory of Evolution in the Business Environment
The critical comparison in this book is the evolution of life forms to businesses. It is that parallel that enables us to compare of the works of Charles Darwin to workforce diversity. The similarities between businesses and living organisms are the critical connections that start the analysis of Charles Darwin's theories and diversity.

There have been hundreds of books and articles written about Charles Darwin's research and books. This book is not written to provide a broad new perspective or a new theory on the works of Charles Darwin. Rather, it is a comparison of the two major works of Charles Darwin to the practice of diversity.

I have great admiration for Darwin's insight to have developed and communicated the theory of evolution, especially given the time period and the basic tools at his disposal. But in reading Charles Darwin's works, I am convinced he had three tools that proved invaluable in his research: a sense for adventure, an open and curious mind, and acute powers of observation.

Darwin's Sense for Adventure
The combination of Charles Darwin's theories to the concept of diversity is rather unique, but there are many similarities and parallels. *On The Origin of Species*, published in 1859, was a groundbreaking and controversial publication at the time. It questioned the origins of existence from the general perspective of nature, not human kind. Darwin's actions represented the quintessential research in biology and diversity. Darwin was raised in a well off family, initially studied medicine at Edinburgh, and later transferred to Cambridge where he took an interest in botany. Rather than choosing the common path of employment, Darwin became the captain's companion and natural historian for the His Majesty's ship, the *Beagle*. It was during this five-year transformative mission that Darwin was exposed to different cultures and species all over the world. Darwin studied nature, conducted research, and kept a detailed diary of his research. This "career path" was quite unique as most men with Darwin's upbringing and education went on to practice medicine, not to sail onboard a ship conducting experiments and closely studying nature for five years. Although Darwin could not have known it, his braveness and boldness would make him famous and virtually a household name decades later.

Darwin's scientific questions and research angered the church as they moved the conversation of creation from a religious discussion to scientific discussion. This was to be expected as the status quo fights back and resists change when questioned. Change is the immortal enemy of the status quo. It is ironic to use the term "status quo" in this discussion as the very term means to prevent change, evolution, or diversification, which is the very thing that enables a life form or a business to adapt or evolve.

DELVING INTO DARWINISM AND DIVERSITY

Darwin's Open and Curious Mind

This brief history is important because it was Darwin's curiosity and open mind that empowered him to study and seek understanding of the biological diversity of nature and man. Darwin did not enter into research and discussions about different cultures and environments with a closed mind and preconceived notions. Darwin took the time and effort to understand a culture and the environment to formulate scientific conclusions. Darwin did not let his perceptions lead him to conclusions; rather, he carefully observed and relied upon the facts to determine the outcome of his research. If Darwin did not approach his research in this manner, we would not have the works of "Charles Darwin" that we have today. *On The Origin of Species and The Descent of Man* would have never been authored and the theory of evolution as we know it would not exist. I believe, however, that the theories that Darwin researched and embraced would have come to light anyway because these theories are so important that they could not be suppressed or ignored.

Five years of research, formulation, and later promoting the theory of evolution could not have been easy for Darwin. In fact, Darwin waited many years after his voyage on the *Beagle* to publish his research in the form of *On The Origin of Species*. Darwin saw many inhabitants of European countries rape and pillage other cultures. While other European researchers were calling aboriginal and Indian natives "savages," you do not see any such conclusions for Darwin in any of his writings. In fact, research indicates Darwin was against slavery. In an age when slavery was the norm, this was an insightful position for Darwin, especially coming from an affluent family. Darwin's five-year voyage on the Beagle, and use of scientific observation to truly understand the diversity of other cultures, their interconnectivity with their natural environment, and the world, is a true exercise in diversity and the seed that created the theory of evolution.

Darwin even uses the word "diversity" a number of times in *On The Origin of Species*; however, this was not what inspired me to connect Darwin to diversity. The first connection was the commonly used phrase "survival of the fittest."

DIVERSIFY OR DIE: DIVERSITY. INCLUSION. EVOLUTION. SUCCESS.

Survival of the Fittest

Charles Darwin's theory of evolution is the backbone in the analysis and study of the advancement of every species, including the human race. This is according to his most popular, and most quoted books, *On The Origin of Species* and *The Descent of Man*.

In *On The Origin of Species*, the fittest survive, and the weakest fail and cease to exist. The common interpretation of this phrase is an over simplification that gives the impression that survival is based on strength or enjoying a high station on the food chain. When in fact, evolutionary survival is based on the diversity in the reproductive and evolutionary process. There are numerous ways living creatures have evolved over the eons. According to Darwin, the fittest survive by slight successive advances on a genetic level that give the species an advantage, and then the advantage is passed down to the offspring. Generations later, the new changes are more pervasive in the community and the species begins to evolve on a higher level. All the while, new advances are occurring and are handed down to the next generation, and then the next generation, making this a continual, never-ending process. Survival of the fittest is a combination of successfully adapting to a changing environment and passing those adaptive traits to offspring.

Natural Selection

Charles Darwin was the first to formulate a scientific argument for the theory of evolution by means of natural selection. Evolution by natural selection is a process that is inferred from three facts about populations:
 1. More offspring are produced than can possibly survive;
 2. Traits vary among individuals, leading to different rates of survival and reproduction; and
 3. Trait differences are heritable.

Thus, when members of a population die, they are replaced by the offspring that are better adapted to survive and reproduce in the environment in which natural selection took place. This process creates and preserves traits that are seemingly fitted for the functional roles they perform. Evolution is not a simple task and generally does not happen overnight. Evolution is usually a long, deliberate process with lots of set backs and failures.

DELVING INTO DARWINISM AND DIVERSITY

Revisiting Darwin in the Business Context

Let's take another look at Darwin's three facts about populations from the perspective of surviving in the business environment. By inserting business phrases into the three laws, we see the applicability of Darwin in the business environment.

1. More businesses are created than can possibly survive;
2. Traits vary among businesses, leading to different rates of survival and business growth; and
3. Trait differences are heritable by successive management chains.

This comparative analysis is important because an organization facing an extremely hostile environment may not have the time or luxury to implement diversity practices or policies to "make sure they get it right" or "make sure they get everyone onboard." There may be occasions where change in the diversity model may need to take place quickly and thoroughly. In these cases, the comparative analysis should not be to humans or mammals but to bacteria and viruses. After all, both bacteria and viruses evolve extremely quickly and are great survivors.

The common denominator in all attempts of evolution is the need to adapt to a changing environment. The changing environment can be based on a change in food and water, change in climate, or new predators.

More Businesses are Created than can Possibly Survive

How does Darwin's theory of evolution relate to business and diversity? It is not that big of a leap actually. The business environment is very competitive and similar to the natural environment—more businesses are created than can be sustained.

Every organization, whether it is a Fortune 500 company, small business, government agency, educational institution, or not for profit, is a combination of different departments and employees that have different functions that must operate in unison for the survival of the organization. Essentially and functionally, that is the same description for a living organism. The only difference is to interchange "departments" or "employees" with "organs" or "cells." For example, if the board of directors is similar to the brains of organizations, then employees are the individual cells. If the board fails to operate effectively, that is similar to the failure of a brain to operate in a living organism. The failure of the brain to operate substantially limits normal biological operations. If the cells fail to operate then the living organism will die, just like a company without employees.

Similarly, if enough employees do not know how to successfully perform their duties, or they make the wrong decisions, or in a worse case scenario engage in illegal activities, the company is exposed to significant legal risk. If this happens, the organization becomes similar to a living organism suffering from cancer where its own cells change, causing serious, sometimes fatal, results. Both of these examples are extreme; after all, a positive environment can impact a business and a living organism just as a negative environment can. A negative environment that contains stress, hard conditions, and extreme competition for limited natural resources could lead to catastrophic results including death—or worse—extinction. For a business, the end result may be bankruptcy, hostile takeover, or going out of business forever.

According to the figures from the Department of Commerce, in 1992, there were 5,095,356 businesses in the United States. In 2011, there were 5,684,424. How does the number of businesses in 2011 support the espoused theory? In 2006, the number of businesses peaked at 6,022,127. In 2006, a massive shift in the business environment put pressure on those businesses so that they could not evolve to the new environmental reality. As a result, 337,703 businesses (5.6%) went out of business between 2006 and 2007. Since 2007, the number of businesses has ranged between 5,930,132 and 5,684,424. They have failed to reach 6,000,000 again.

These figures only represent the businesses that are incorporated or submit their data to the census bureau. If you want to look at the local business environment, a drive around your neighborhood to see all of the "for sale," "for lease," or "for rent" signs would give you an idea of how local businesses have been evolving to face the challenging business environment.

In a 2013 article entitled "The Stock Market is Shrinking Despite Record High Indexes," Michael Santoli reports, "there are fewer publicly traded companies on American exchanges than at any time since at least 1990." The article goes on to state:

> *The total number of US exchange-listed companies peaked near 8,800 in 1997 and has since sunk to 4,900 as of year-end 2012, according to data furnished by Strategas Group. The ranks of public companies declined slowly into the 2000 market peak and then entered a steep downtrend in the early- and mid-2000s.*
>
> *De-listings of failed uncompetitive technology stocks, another M&A surge in the mid-2000s, and a relative shortage of initial stock offerings all contributed.*

Santoli's analysis is consistent with the Department of Commerce data as both statistics show businesses suffering from the harsh business environment in the mid-2000s. This information also shows how a harsh business environment can cause a business to face extinction.

The analysis of the harsh business environment does not only exist in multi-year analysis, it also exists on a month-to-month basis. According to *Forbes*, approximately 543,000 new businesses get started each month, but more employer businesses shut down than start up each month. According to *Bloomberg.com*, eight out of ten entrepreneurs who start businesses fail within the first eighteen months, mostly because they run out of cash. That is an 80% rate of failure. The vast majority of these businesses are small businesses that do not have the resources or the need to create a "diversity and inclusion department"; however, this data continues to support the position that businesses are subject to the Darwinism of survival, evolution, and extinction.

Traits Vary, Leading to Different Rates of Survival and Organizational Growth

It is impossible to discuss all of the traits that lead to the survival and growth of an organization. One general way to identify the difference in traits is to identify organizational differences. The question becomes: What constitutes "organizational differences"?

DIVERSIFY OR DIE: DIVERSITY. INCLUSION. EVOLUTION. SUCCESS.

According to an article in *The Harvard Business Review (HBR)*, "the most profitable strategies are built on differentiation: offering customers something they value that competitors don't have" ("Discovering New Points of Differentiation," 1997). An analysis of the author's two-step process within the context of diversity follows: mapping the consumption chain, and analyzing your customer's experience and focused creativity.

1. Mapping the Consumption Chain

In the first step, the author recommends mapping the customer's experience with product or service with each customer segment. The inclusion of diversity should be an important component of this "mapping process." In order to completely understand your customer's experience, you have to view their experience from their culture. Some marketing examples from *essentialaction.org* illustrate this point:

- General Motors had a problem when they introduced the Chevy Nova in South America. Despite their best efforts, they weren't selling many cars. They finally realized that in Spanish, "nova" means, "it won't go." Sales improved dramatically after the car was renamed the "Caribe."
- The Dairy Association's huge success with the campaign "Got Milk?" prompted them to expand advertising to Mexico. It was soon brought to their attention the Spanish translation read: "Are you Lactating?"
- When Kentucky Fried Chicken entered the Chinese market, to their horror they discovered that their slogan "finger lickin' good" came out as: "eat your fingers off."

These examples showcase the importance of understanding your customer's culture in the marketing phase. The total customer service experience goes well beyond marketing. In *Crafting the Customer Service Experience for People Not Like You: How to Delight and Engage the Customers You Don't Understand,* author Kelly McDonald recognizes and acknowledges the growing diversity customer community and the importance of beneficially controlling the customer service experience. An organization that recognizes and evolves to the needs of the customer with their culture in mind sets itself apart from its competition.

2. Analyzing your Customer's Experience

The second step in "Discovering New Points of Differentiation" advocates analyzing the customers experience after use of the product or service. The *HBR* article recommends using a five-question analysis based on the following categories: what, where, who, when, and how. The most insightful part to this step, however, is the section on "focused creativity."

The article comments on how the failure of a company to focus the creativity and imagination of its employees results in a failure to benefit from their employment. Indeed, large organizations may even limit their creativity and imagination by applying "homogeneous pressures." The author closes the article with this powerful insight.

Although "Discovering New Points of Differentiation" was written in 1997, the application in the current day is more important than it was then. Advances in technology, communications, and the increased speed in which funding can be raised and products brought to market are light years faster than 1997. In addition, the demographics of the United States have evolved, resulting in a dramatically different and far more multicultural customer base. These differences require a heightened focus on creativity and imagination than foreseen in 1997. In this current, evolving business environment, "homogeneous pressures" increase the odds of "homogeneous extinction."

Trait Differences are Heritable by Successive Management Chains

Managers are usually in very influential positions. Many employees look to managers for leadership and may even view them as role models. Whenever I train managers, I inform them that employees are constantly paying attention to what they say and even more attention to their managerial actions. This is especially true for senior executives as they set the tone for the entire organization. Bad management styles, ideals, and principles are likely passed down to, or inherited by, future managers and pose a threat to the evolution of the organization, increasing the chances of extinction.

Similar to the title and opening statement "diversify or die," this argument may seem dramatic, but poor management decisions and communications have caused thousands of lawsuits that would not have happened without the poor management decisions.

The Inhibitors of Evolution

Darwin felt evolution was the key to the long-term success of a species; however, this was not the viewpoint of all in the scientific and religious community. Darwin's theories created enemies, so much so that it took decades for his theory of evolution to gain acceptance. For example, Richard Owen, a scientist who had significant weight in the scientific community at the time was an outspoken opponent of the theory of evolution. Similar to the viewpoint of the church, Owen felt evolution was based on "divine guidance" and predicted Darwin's work would be forgotten in ten years. Who is Richard Owen you ask? Exactly.

As the theory of evolution had its enemies, so does the business case for diversity. The similarities between the concept of diversity and the theory of evolution will also have enemies. In the business environment, there are numerous enemies to diversity and evolution:

- Managers and executives who wish to maintain a balance of power.
- Employees who want the "status quo" to remain unchanged.
- Outdated policies and practices.
- Adherence to prior investment in technology thus preventing investment in future technologies.
- Failure to invest in training.

All of these enemies of evolution have caused many companies to stumble, even fail. However, in the field of diversity, there is one enemy of evolution that merits specific discussion: Business leaders and middle managers in companies who do not want to implement diversity efforts or policies.

These business leaders and managers:
- Question the legitimacy of diversity.
- Object to the concept of diversity.
- Remain quiet because they know diversity is a political hot potato.
- Support the ideals of diversity in words but not actions.

DELVING INTO DARWINISM AND DIVERSITY

One of the lessons I have learned over the many years engaged in the practice of diversity is that business leaders and managers who refuse to believe in the principles and benefits of diversity based on affirmative action and EEO do not want to change their minds. Ironically, these same people are very capable of changing their minds on many other topics.

I have heard the excuse "they are set in their ways" many times, but they have managed to change in every other way of their life. These are the same people who have accepted the transition from the use of the landline telephone for communication to video conferencing, from US Postal Service to e-mail and social media, from door-to-door sales to online sales, and from a US-based manufacturing of products to outsourcing and overseas manufacturing. Why is it that the thought process can evolve on so many other levels, but not diversity?

Then, as you can guess by the title of the book, the next question is, "What happens when you choose to live in the past and not recognize, let alone embrace, the current state of diversity?" Diversify or die.

Evolve and Succeed:
- Analyze your consumption chain from the cultural perspective. If specific goods or services are not selling, a cultural analysis may provide insight and improve sales. Be honest to this process by creating the analysis from the actual perspective of the culture, not *your* perspective of the culture.
- Understand that your current managers are most likely grooming your future managers for leadership. If your current managers are enemies of evolution, it is likely your future managers will adopt the same perspective. Will your organization evolve if the managers, as enemies of evolution, create more enemies of evolution?

CHAPTER 3

THE DIVERSITY EQUATION AND DEFINITION OF "DIVERSITY AND INCLUSION"

"The truth of the principle, that the greatest amount of life can be supported by great diversification of structure, is seen under many natural circumstances. In an extremely small area, especially if freely open to immigration, and where the contest between individual and individual must be severe, we always find great diversity in its inhabitants."

— Charles Darwin *On The Origin of Species*

A few years ago, I was in a three-day training with a number of midlevel diversity managers and directors studying to become Certified Diversity Executives. During our many discussions about diversity, I asked a critical question: "How do each of you define 'diversity'? In all of my years of managing and consulting on diversity, I never thought to directly ask this question to a group of diversity practitioners.

Every participant had a different perspective and definition of diversity. As we continued the discussion around the definition of diversity, no one was willing to fully accept anyone else's definition. Although we all agreed in theory that diversity is required for a company to increase profits and create an inclusive, efficient, and productive workforce, a singular definition of diversity escaped our group. At the end of the exercise, we agreed in principle about the definition of diversity, but not in wording.

Upon reflection of this discussion, it occurred to me that the failure to reach consensus on a definition would not have occurred if the topics were traditional corporate business concepts or departments. For example, the definitions of sales, marketing, safety, legal, and human resources are very established, and therefore, very uniform. This distinction presents one of diversity's greatest strengths and simultaneously one of diversity's greatest challenges.

The subjective nature and definition of diversity gives CEOs and diversity executives the latitude to create their own definition of diversity and subsequent policies and practices to support that definition. Further, even if the CEO sets forth a credible definition of diversity, it is possible that many employees may not agree with the definition. This disconnect can impact the principle and practice of diversity on many levels.

The nature of the definition of diversity results in debates and disagreements about the concepts, principles, and practices related to diversity. When this debate occurs between diversity professionals, the debate does not take away or diminish the concept or importance of diversity. Like my diversity executive colleagues, diversity professionals are in agreement in principle about the benefits of diversity. However, when the diversity debate occurs among those who don't support diversity, the lack of a uniform definition often results in negative and counter-productive conversations. The ability to use diversity to influence business decisions is weakened by the lack of uniformity and consistency.

Definitions of Diversity

Let's look at a few definitions of diversity, taken directly from their sources, and see how they differ:
- The United States Government—We define workforce diversity as a collection of individual attributes that together help agencies pursue organizational objectives efficiently and effectively. These include, but are not limited to, characteristics such as national origin, language, race, color, disability, ethnicity, gender, age, religion, sexual orientation, gender identity, socioeconomic status, veteran status, and family structures. The concept also encompasses differences among people concerning where they are from and where they have lived and their difference of thought and life experiences.
- Society for Human Resource Management (SHRM)—The collective mixture of differences and similarities that includes for example,

individual and organizational characteristics, values, beliefs, experiences, backgrounds, preferences, and behaviors.
- Dr. Roosevelt Thomas (1944 – 2013, Author, Thought Leader, and Champion of Diversity) — Any collective mixture characterized by differences, similarities, and related tensions and complexities.
- Dictionary.com—The inclusion of individuals representing more than one national origin, color, religion, socioeconomic stratum, sexual orientation, etc.
- BusinessDictionary.com—Similarities and differences among employees in terms of age, cultural background, physical abilities and disabilities, race, religion, sex, and sexual orientation.
- United Way—The quality of being different or unique at the individual or group level. This includes age; ethnicity; gender; gender identity; language differences; nationality; parental status; physical, mental and developmental abilities; race; religion; sexual orientation; skin color; socio-economic status; work and behavioral styles; the perspectives of each individual shaped by their nation, experiences and culture—and more. Even when people appear the same on the outside, they are different!
- The George Washington University—The term diversity is used to describe individual differences (e.g., life experiences, learning and working styles, personality types) and group/social differences (e.g., race, socio-economic status, class, gender, sexual orientation, country of origin, ability, intellectual traditions and perspectives, as well as cultural, political, religious, and other affiliations) that can be engaged to achieve excellence in teaching, learning, research, scholarship, and administrative and support services.
- The American Alliance of Museums—The quality of being different or unique at the individual or group level. This includes age; ethnicity; gender; gender identity; language differences; nationality; parental status; physical, mental, and developmental abilities; race; religion; sexual orientation; skin color; socio-economic status; education; work and behavioral styles; the perspectives of each individual shaped by their nation, experiences, and culture—and more. Even when people appear the same on the outside, they are different.

Enter Inclusion

Inclusion is a strategy to leverage diversity. Diversity always exists in social systems; inclusion, on the other hand, must be created. In order to leverage diversity, the employer must create a workplace where employees feel supported, listened to, and able to do their best work.

In order for diversity and inclusion to have an effect on an organization, diversity measures must be identified and tracked. Here are some of the measures an employer can track to determine the impact of diversity efforts:
- Improved bottom line
- Increased on return on investment
- Increased sales
- Improved cost effectiveness
- Access to new markets
- More products or services
- More diverse student body
- More diverse faculty
- Increased donations
- Whatever positive impact diversity can have on your organization

When all three components of diversity are included in the definition, the impact on the organization is clearer and directly related to the mission of the organization.

Definitions of inclusion taken directly from the same sources as the definitions of diversity listed above include:
- The United States Government—We define inclusion as a culture that connects each employee to the organization; encourages collaboration, flexibility, and fairness; and leverages diversity throughout the organization so that all individuals are able to participate and contribute to their full potential.
- Society for Human Resource Management (SHRM)—The achievement of a work environment in which all individuals are treated fairly and respectfully, have equal access to opportunities and resources, and can contribute fully to the organization's success.

DIVERSIFY OR DIE: DIVERSITY. INCLUSION. EVOLUTION. SUCCESS.

- Dr. Roosevelt Thomas (1944 – 2013, Author, Thought Leader, and Champion of Diversity)—RThomasConsulting.com does not expressly define inclusion.
- Dictionary.com—1. The act of including. 2. The state of being included. 3. Something that is included.
- BusinessDictionary.com—Does not have a definition on inclusion.
- United Way—The collective mixture of differences and similarities that includes for example, individual and organizational characteristics, values, beliefs, experiences, backgrounds, preferences, and behaviors.
- The George Washington University—The term inclusion is used to describe the active, intentional, and ongoing engagement with diversity—in people, in the curriculum, in the co-curriculum, and in communities (e.g., intellectual, social, cultural, geographic) with which individuals might connect.
- The American Alliance of Museums—The act of including; a strategy to leverage diversity.

The lack of a definition of diversity and inclusion is compounded by the fact there are separate and independent definitions for diversity and inclusion. In order for diversity and inclusion to evolve, the definitions of diversity and inclusion must be combined into one definition that provides focus and clarity for the organization.

A clear and complete definition of diversity must have three components. First, the definition must reference cultural and socio-economic differences. Second, the definition must relate the cultural and socio-economic differences to the organization. The third, and perhaps the most important component, which is not in all of the above reference definitions of diversity or inclusion is "substantial relevance to the organization."

In a definition of diversity that positively impacts an organization, all three components are required for an effective definition for diversity. An effective method to analyze the definitions of diversity is to disassemble the definitions into their component parts and analyze each component.

THE DIVERSITY EQUATION

The first equation for diversity:
Statement of cultural identities = definition of diversity

The second equation for diversity:
Cultural identities + substantial relevance to the organization = definition of diversity

Here is the third equation for diversity:
Cultural identities + substantial relevance to the organization + impact on organizational effectiveness = definition of diversity

All equations recognize cultural identities such as:
- Race,
- Gender,
- National origin,
- Culture,
- Color,
- Religion,
- Disability,
- LGBT,
- Veteran status,
- Generational status (traditionalists, baby boomers, genXers, genYers, and millennials),
- Educational background, and
- Any category that can be considered a culture.

In addition, the last two equations recognize substantial relevance to the organization.

The first "equation" is more of a statement. In mathematical terms, it is saying "4 = 4." The first diversity equation does not help an organization in using diversity to evolve. The second diversity equation helps as it states how diversity helps an organization evolve. Both equations are missing the third component: the "impact on organizational effectiveness." This is where "inclusion" from "diversity and inclusion" enters the equation. For clarity, from this point on the "third equation for diversity" is the "diversity equation."

DIVERSIFY OR DIE: DIVERSITY. INCLUSION. EVOLUTION. SUCCESS.

The Evolution of a Definition

Let's put the diversity equation to work and create an effective definition of diversity that can be used in every organization. For the purposes of this book, diversity and inclusion does not include supplier diversity. While supplier diversity is an important business practice with critical economic implications to minority- and female-owned businesses, supplier diversity is a related, but separate concept in the analysis. Also, "diversity and inclusion" stated together make up the most common reference to diversity efforts, unless stated otherwise for the rest of the book, the singular reference to diversity also means diversity and inclusion.

For the purposes of this book, and for your organization if you choose, diversity is generally defined as:

The business practice to increase the bottom line by capitalizing on the responsible sale and distribution of goods or services to multicultural clientele and the supportive employment of multicultural employees at all levels of the organization.

This definition of diversity clearly communicates the positive and powerful impact diversity can have on the three most important factors for a business: profit, loss, and employees. The core of this definition is focused around the bottom line, the sale of goods and services, and the resources used to support the sale of goods and services. This definition takes diversity out of the world of compliance and into the world of successful business practices where it belongs and has the greatest impact on an organization.

Responsible Sale of Goods and Services

Why is the clause "the responsible sale of goods and services" included in the definition? The diversity community—specifically, African Americans, Latinos, Asians, and Native Americans—has over a trillion-dollar impact on the US economy. Latinos are the fastest growing racial group in the United States. Depending on the product or service, these racial and ethnic groups are potential clients and customers that serve as major sources of revenue.

Organizations that are prepared to evolve realize the sale of goods and services to the diversity community increases the bottom line. In banking for example, fifteen years ago English was the only language option on ATMs outside of major cities. Now, Spanish has been included on the vast majority of ATM machines. Some ATM machines have up to ten language options. This is just one example of how diversity has positively impacted banking business practices.

Unfortunately, unethical companies have marketed and sold products and services to the diversity communities for more money or at higher interest rates for one reason: to unfairly and illegally profit off of them. The most recent example was the sale of mortgages to the diversity community, primarily to the African American and Latino community. The dramatic increase of home ownership seemed like a wonderful opportunity at the time; however, history shows it was greedy, irresponsible, shortsighted, and one of the precursors to the mortgage and financial meltdown.

Many African Americans and Latinos purchased homes with mortgages with adjustable rates, higher interest rates, or higher fees compared to other segments of the population. Many African Americans and Latinos were sold these mortgages even though they qualified for fixed rate mortgages or for a lower interest rate. Yet, during this time of the "housing boom" if you had asked these mortgage brokers and bankers about their service to the diversity community, they would have told you they were helping the diversity community live the "American dream."

The greedy and unethical actions of the mortgage brokers and bankers started a chain of events that resulted in a record number of foreclosures, and played an important role in the US mortgage and financial meltdown that had international impact. Of course, all of the blame for the mortgage crisis is not on mortgage brokers and bankers; the mortgage crisis was worsened by mortgage-backed securities.

There are many documented reasons why "the responsible sale of goods and services" is so important to the definition of diversity. As an avid reader and researcher of issues related to diversity and inclusion, I was aware of many settlements and judgments related to discriminatory practices in the sale of goods and services. However, when I combined the largest judgments and settlements, I was shocked and disappointed.

Bank of America: $335 Million

Bank of America paid a record $335 million to settle civil charges that it discriminated against minority homebuyers. The banking giant agreed to the payout following an investigation into the policies of Countrywide, a company that specialized in so-called subprime mortgages and focused on loans to those with lower credit ratings. Bank of America bought out Countrywide in 2008. Countrywide customers were charged higher interest rates and monthly mortgage payments that suddenly increased after two or three years of home ownership.

Countrywide also steered minorities to more expensive subprime loans even though they were qualified for traditional mortgage rates. US Justice Department officials report it was the largest residential discrimination settlement in US history.

Capital One: $2.85 Million

Capital One paid $2.85 million in damages to settle allegations that Chevy Chase Bank, which it purchased on 2009, charged African American and Hispanic mortgage seekers higher interest rates and fees than white borrowers for no other reason that their race and national origin.

Other examples of unethical and illegal wrong doing along with financial impact include:

Insurance Policies: $556 Million

Sixteen major insurance policy cases were settled between 2000 and 2004. These cases covered 14.8 million policies sold by ninety insurance companies between 1900 and the 1980s. Together, the settlements required the companies to pay more than $556 million—most of it to pay back policyholders or their survivors. The two biggest settlements: American General Life and Accident Insurance Co., of Nashville, TN, agreed in 2000 to pay $250 million in a case involving 9.1 million policies. Metropolitan Life Insurance Co. of New York agreed in 2002 to pay $157 million for 1.9 million policies.

THE DIVERSITY EQUATION

Texaco: $176 Million
In 1996, Texaco settled the largest racial discrimination federal lawsuit where 1,400 black employees alleged they were denied promotions based on race. This case received a great deal of media attention due to a secret recording on a senior executive meeting where the attendees used racial slurs, poked fun at Kwanzaa, and threatened to destroy documents the court demanded in the lawsuit.

Auto Loans: $80 Million
The Consumer Financial Protection Bureau (CFPB) and Department of Justice (DOJ) ordered Ally Financial Inc. and Ally Bank (Ally) to pay $80 million in damages to harmed African American, Hispanic, Asian, and Pacific Islander borrowers, and $18 million in penalties. The CFPB and DOJ determined that more than 235,000 minority borrowers paid higher interest rates for their auto loans between April 2011 and December 2013 because of Ally's discriminatory pricing system.

Denny's Restaurants: $54 Million
In 1994, Denny's Restaurants agreed to pay $54 million dollars to settle lawsuits filed by black customers. The black customers alleged they had to wait longer for service, were refused service, were forced to prepay for their meals, and were treated rudely by Denny's employees.

Auto Loans: $18 Million
Fifth Third Bank paid an $18 million settlement to resolve allegations that they discriminated against African American and Hispanic borrowers in its indirect auto lending business. Thousands of African American and Hispanic customers paid over $200 more on auto loans over the course of the loan than white customers.

Auto Insurance: $6 Million
Insurance giant GEICO, Government Employees Insurance Company, paid $6 million to settle a complaint accusing the company of unfairly over charging poor, low-and-moderate income women, and single drivers. GEICO charged those targeted drivers as much as 54 percent more than other good drivers for a minimum-limits policy.

United States Postal Service: $4.5 Million
The United States Postal Service (USPS) settled a discrimination suit where employees with hearing problems were not given proper technologies and services to help them perform their duties.

The City of Chicago: $3.7 Million
The City of Chicago settled a class action lawsuit where female firefighters claimed that the firefighter test was not related to job performance and was used to discourage potential new female firefighters.

Honda Auto Loans: Multi-Million Dollar Settlement
In 2015, carmaker Honda settled a multi-million dollar lawsuit for charging higher rates to African Americans and Latinos.

General Overcharge for Contraceptives
In 2014, CVS violated the Affordable Care Act (ACA) by overcharging thousands of women for generic contraceptives that should have been provided at no extra cost (*Huffington Post*, 2014). The ACA requires that any FDA-approved form of birth control, including the pill, IUDs, or patches, be provided without cost sharing as long as the patient has a doctor's prescription.

The total bill for these twelve lawsuits: over $1.2 billion. This cost does not even include attorneys' fees, loss in productivity, and lowered employee morale. This is a good example of the pain that can be avoided as discussed earlier in Chapter 1—$1.2 billion is a lot of pain.

The Final Component, the Multicultural Employee
Finally, the definition of diversity contains the term: "multicultural employee." It is important to note that the term "culture" is a much broader term than race, ethnicity, and gender. It is the intent of this definition that the "multicultural" employee is not a legal or compliance term that only addresses the classes covered in Title VII or Executive Orders 8802, 11246, or 11375, but covers many of the classes of people that diversity has been known to cover.

Multicultural refers to: race, gender, national origin, culture, color, age (young or old), religion, disability, LGBT, veteran status, generational status (traditionalists, baby boomers, genXers, genYers, and millennials), educational background, and any category that can be considered a culture.

The Definition of Diversity for Not for Profits
How does the definition relate to not for profits, churches, and colleges/universities? *Diversify or Die* uses the term "organization" rather than "company" to make sure the evolutionary principles of diversity addressed in the book extend to many types of organizations. The words "the bottom line," rather than "profits" were carefully chosen to make this definition useful in the broadest spectrum on organizations. After all, not for profits, churches, and colleges/universities all have a bottom line.

The use of diversity and inclusion is generally the same for all organizations. So how can the effective use of diversity positively impact your bottom line? Using the diversity equation, a not for profit can create a definition for diversity that uses language with closer ties to the not for profit environment:

The business practice to obtain sustained funding, resources, and volunteers to provide services to a multicultural community and the supportive employment of multicultural employees at all levels of the organization.

This diversity definition serves not for profit organizations as "funding" can refer to: donations, grants, program income, and sponsorships. Similarly, "resources" can refer to: in-kind donations, pro-bono work, and many other ways educational institutions and not for profits can increase the success of a not for profit. How does this definition translate to "impact on organizational effectiveness" in the equation? By using diversity and inclusion to:
- Increase donations
- Increase resources
- Increase volunteers

Once the definition of diversity is directly linked to the objectives of the organization, the equation is also linked to the bottom line.

DIVERSIFY OR DIE: DIVERSITY. INCLUSION. EVOLUTION. SUCCESS.

The Definition of Diversity for Educational Institutions
Colleges and universities have unique diversity and inclusion challenges. The business of education is very different than most other products or services, so the definition of diversity has to reflect those differences.

The business practice to provide excellent centers of learning to a multicultural student body and the employment of multicultural professors, administrators, and staff at all levels of the educational institution.

For educational institutions, this definition covers "centers of learning." The best practice of all centers of learning is to recruit the best teachers and administrators to recruit and teach the best students. "Centers of learning" also includes publications to increase the external level of academic excellence.

The definition of diversity for educational institutions also specifically includes "multicultural professors, administrators, and staff." The visibility of these employees and the inclusion of diverse points of view are beneficial to the learning environment.

The Definition of Diversity for Small Businesses
Large organizations are not the only organizations that can benefit from diversity and inclusion; small businesses can benefit as well. Diversity and inclusion can be the most difficult for small businesses because most of them have to use every penny and every credit dollar to continue to operate.

Many small businesses do not have a human resources department or in-house counsel to run a diversity program. Unless the small business has government contracts over $50,000, they are not required to use affirmative action in the hiring, retention, and promotion of employees. But, diversity is still extremely important to small businesses. In fact, diversity may give small organizations the advantage over the competition in a rapidly evolving market.

A real estate broker is a good example of a small business. In 2016, I had an insightful discussion with an older white male realtor about the diversity of his clients. When selling a house to a millennial, he responds the same way they contact him. Gone are the days of always calling your client. If the millennial client sends an e-mail, the realtor responds with an e-mail. If the millennial client calls the realtor, the realtor responds with a return call. If the millennial client sends a text, the realtor responds with a text. I was not surprised when the realtor laughed while telling me he has texted more in the last year than he has in his entire life. This is a small businessman who has evolved with diversity.

Imagine if his position was "the only way to do business is to talk on the phone or meet face to face. If we are not doing that, we are not doing business. This new technology is not business." Sound familiar? Everyone knows someone like that. In business, that point of view is an express train to extinction.

The business practice to increase the bottom line by capitalizing on the responsible sale and distribution of goods or services to multicultural clientele and the supportive employment of multicultural employees at all levels of the organization.

Sound familiar? This is the original definition of diversity. Why is the definition the same as the original definition? Because the main difference between a Fortune 500 company and a small business is size and scale. Otherwise, both businesses are designed to do the same thing—make a profit.

Most small businesses do not view diversity as a profit-generating tool. Continuing with our parallel between Darwin and diversity, the greatest amount of businesses can be supported by diversification of business structure and interests. If the difference is size and scale, then the difference is the way the small business applies the practice of diversity and inclusion. Measurement of diversity and inclusion programs is even more important to a small business. With a much smaller profit margin, diversity and inclusion programs must directly and effectively improve the bottom line of the small business to justify the continued investment in diversity and inclusion.

The Definition of Diversity and Inclusion for Government Agencies
Diversity and inclusion is inherent for government operations. The founding

DIVERSIFY OR DIE: DIVERSITY. INCLUSION. EVOLUTION. SUCCESS.

fathers set up an extremely diverse government on all levels to ensure checks and balances and the distribution of power to "form a more perfect union." Diversity of government based on the three branches—executive, legislative, and judicial—as well as federal powers versus state powers provide the structure for the operation of our government and country. So how does the US government definition of diversity compare to the diversity equation and subsequently the definition of diversity?

The US government definition of diversity references cultural identities and substantial relevance to the organization, but like many definitions, does not address "impact on organizational effectiveness." Unlike corporations, not for profits, and educational institutions, the government is not in the business of producing a profit. Taxpayer dollars are collected to finance the government, and even so, the government can operate under a deficit for many years. While there are few government agencies that have the ability to raise money (the Internal Revenue Service and the Postal Service come to mind), it begs the question: what is the currency to which diversity can be measured in the US government? The US government diversity currency includes: laws/policy, diplomacy, protection of intellectual property, and customer service.

Tax Dollars at Work for Diversity
Based on organizational effectiveness, a proposed definition of diversity and inclusion for any government agency reads as follows:

The civil duty for agencies to fulfill government charters and create, interpret, and enforce laws and policies in a sound and responsible manner for a multicultural population and the supportive employment of multicultural employees at all levels of the agency.

The introduction of a comprehensive uniform definition is the first step in the continuation of the evolution of diversity. Charles Darwin at work.

"Diversity of Thought"
One of the latest catch phrases in the field of diversity is the "diversity of thought." Diversity of thought is stating that diversity and inclusion is more than race, gender, ethnicity, culture, and sexual orientation. Under diversity

of thought, diversity is a principle. If we think in a "diverse manner" all of the other historical, previously used forms of diversity are not needed anymore.

Even in a perfect world, or a world without discrimination, diversity of thought cannot work by itself because no one can totally think in the perspectives of all other races, genders, cultures, or sexual orientations. Diversity of thought does not address many issues that diversity addresses. For example, diversity of thought does not address:
- Managing employees based on their diverse backgrounds
- Managing Employee Resource Groups
- Managing Diversity Councils
- Product development for different languages, cultures, or diverse communities
- Marketing products or services to different languages, cultures, or diverse communities to improve sales

When an organization is looking to improve sales, donations, or tuition-based students, and wants to market and sell to the diversity market, just using the magic words diversity of thought will not work. Diversity of thought is only the beginning of the diversity and inclusion process. If an organization uses diversity of thought as the end of the diversity and inclusion process, it will move diversity and inclusion efforts in the wrong direction.

Why does diversity of thought move organizations in the wrong direction? One reason is because diversity of thought does not provide numbers to measure diversity successes or failures. How do you measure thought? Without actual numbers to measure progress, diversity of thought is a simple phrase that does not add measurable value to diversity and inclusion.

Diversity of thought may work in one way. If diversity of thought is used as a means to embrace, enhance, or improve current or future quantifiable diversity initiatives, then diversity of thought may a good first step. If presented in a structured environment, diversity of thought is a useful way to engage employees to think out of the box, but in any scenario, diversity of thought is a beginning, not the end.

DIVERSIFY OR DIE: DIVERSITY. INCLUSION. EVOLUTION. SUCCESS.

The Next Step in the Evolution of Diversity

In a business environment, evolution is the adaption and use of the "new" rather than the relying on the "old."

The events that cause evolution need not be broad or profound; one purpose or event can cause a chain of events that lead to evolution. Examples of events that Darwin used include: change in climate, change in food source, and introduction of a new species into an ecosystem.

Events that lead to evolution or extinction in the business environment are all around us. Some companies will survive, most will not. In an article in the USA Today dated December 23, 2014, there are ten industries that are facing extinction in the US:

  10. Online mortgage brokers
   9. Database & directory publishing
   8. Body armor manufacturing
   7. Men's & boys' apparel manufacturing
   6. DVD, game & video rental
   5. Data recovery services
   4. Tank and armored vehicles manufacturing
   3. Wind turbine installation
   2. Computer manufacturing
   1. Recordable media manufacturing

Clearly, the evolution in technology and manufacturing is threatening the extinction of these industries; but this is not the end of the evolutionary analysis. There are many evolutionary pressures in every industry. The question is: how can you use diversity to help your organization evolve?

Evolve and Succeed

- How does your organization define diversity compared to the diversity equation?
- Are all of the components of the diversity equation present in your definition of diversity?
- How is your industry evolving? Are you evolving with your industry or using the business practices of yesterday to compete with the market of tomorrow?

CHAPTER 4
A MODERN SOCIO-ECONOMIC HISTORY OF DIVERSITY

"On the theory of natural selection the extinction of old forms and the production of new and improved forms are intimately connected together."

— Charles Darwin *On The Origin of Species*

An evolutionary analysis is important to demonstrate the close connections between the old forms of diversity and the new, improved forms of diversity. The timeline is one way to connect the extinction of an old form and the production of a new one.

Timelines compare the environment, tools, and technology used to survive at multiple points in the past to those used in the present. One of the objectives of the timeline is to understand the evolution from one point to another. Timelines are important tools to analyze key points from the past and shed light on the possibilities of the future.

A timeline analysis can also apply to diversity. The factors and events that started the concept of diversity, before it was even called "diversity," have advanced through important events to evolve principles and practices of diversity. It is impossible to acknowledge all of the events that led to the evolution of diversity, as many events are regional, local, or occur within an organization. The diversity events on the timeline presented here are on a very broad scale as they have impacted millions, if not billions.

DIVERSIFY OR DIE: DIVERSITY. INCLUSION. EVOLUTION. SUCCESS.

Many organizations have published timelines of historic events related to diversity. Some of these diversity timelines include events as far back as the Jim Crow era. While all of these events have historical significance, they do not focus on the evolution of diversity from a socio-economic perspective. This chapter presents a modern day history of diversity from a socio-economic perspective to illustrate how diversity has evolved in the past fifty years. Many of the diversity events in this timeline are not well known, and are not the usual entries included in diversity timelines. All of the entries, however, played an important role in modern business history and socio-economic history.

A Few Important Historical Events

While this timeline is exclusively based on events that occurred in the US, it should be noted that many Fortune 500 companies listed in the timeline have subsidiaries or major centers of business in other countries, which directly incorporates US diversity into the business world of other counties.

As this is a modern day socio-economic analysis, historical events are beyond the scope of this analysis. However, a few historic and socio-economic events should be recognized to show that historical events did not start with the first entry in the diversity timeline.
- In June 1888, abolitionist Frederick Douglass received one vote from the Kentucky delegation at the Republican convention in Chicago, effectively making him the first black candidate to have his name placed in nomination for president of the United States.
- In 1908, "Black Wall Street" was founded in the Greenwood neighborhood in Tulsa, Oklahoma. (Though in 1912, Black Wall Street was destroyed in a race riot that killed 300 and left 4,300 homeless.)

Evolutionary Diversity Timeline Methodology

All of the entries in the evolutionary diversity timeline have at least one of the following:
- Past, present, or future of the buying power in the diversity community by group
- Legal cases with significant economic or policy impact

A MODERN SOCIO-ECONOMIC HISTORY OF DIVERSITY

- Social trends and predictions that have an immediate socio-economic impact on diversity
- Ground breaking performances and successes of diversity businesses
- Major business accomplishments, mergers, and acquisitions

In the spirit of the Darwin quote for this chapter, the timeline shows the improvement, evolution, and progression of diversity and inclusion by showing how the present has been built off of the successes of the past. This evolutionary diversity timeline is also important from a generational perspective. Many traditionalists and baby boomers have lived these events and remember them quite well. To these generations, these events are parts of their past not historical events. There are new generations of employees that only view diversity from the time they entered the workplace after 2000. A historical perspective may prove useful in helping the newer workforce appreciate the depth and breadth of diversity and inclusion.

Evolutionary Diversity Timeline

1941—President Roosevelt issues Executive Order 8802 banning discrimination against minorities in defense contracts.

1942—John H. Johnson borrows $500 for seed money that created Johnson Publishing Co., home of Ebony and Jet magazines. Johnson was placed on the Forbes 400 list of the nation's wealthiest citizens.

1954—In Brown v. Board of Education, the United States Supreme Court rules that deliberate public school segregation is illegal and states that schools must be desegregated with all deliberate speed.

1954—In Hernandez v. Texas, the United States Supreme Court rules that Hispanics have equal protection under the Fourteenth Amendment.

1954—WKAQ-TV launches the "Telemundo" brand in San Juan, Puerto Rico.

DIVERSIFY OR DIE: DIVERSITY. INCLUSION. EVOLUTION. SUCCESS.

1955—Raul Cortez founds KCOR-TV (now KWEX-DT) in San Antonio, Texas, which, through a series of transactions, was renamed Univision in 1986.

1961—President John F. Kennedy signs Executive Order 10925 requiring that government employers not discriminate against any employee based on race, creed, color, or national origin.

1963—The March on Washington takes place where the Reverend Dr. Martin Luther King Jr. delivers his famous "I Have a Dream" speech.

1964—Congress passes the Civil Rights Act, which protects citizens against discrimination and segregation.

1965—President Johnson issues Executive Order 11246 requiring federal agencies and contractors to use "affirmative action" in hiring minorities to overcome employment discrimination.

1966—The National Organization of Women (NOW) is founded to advocate for political equality for women.

1967—President Johnson expands Executive Order 11375 to include women in non-discrimination efforts.

1967—Congress passes the Age Discrimination in Employment Act (ADEA) that prohibits discrimination against workers on a federal level that are forty years or older.

1967—President Lyndon Johnson appoints Thurgood Marshall to the United States Supreme Court. Thurgood Marshall is the first African American appointed to the Supreme Court.

1969—The Minority Business Development Agency (MBDA) is founded by President Richard Nixon. MBDA is an agency of the US Department of Commerce that helps to create and sustain

A MODERN SOCIO-ECONOMIC HISTORY OF DIVERSITY

US jobs by promoting the growth and global competitiveness of businesses owned and operated by minority entrepreneurs.

1969—The Gay Rights Movement starts in New York City.

1970—Earl Graves Sr. starts Earl G. Graves, Ltd., and under that holding company, he starts the Earl G. Graves Associates Management Consulting Firm. In August 1970, the first issue of Black Enterprise magazine was published.

1972—Title IX is added to the Education Amendment prohibiting discrimination based on gender in educational programs that receive federal assistance.

1972—Katharine Graham becomes the first female Fortune 500 CEO, as CEO of The Washington Post.

1974—Congress passes the Vocational Rehabilitation Act (Rehab Act) barring discrimination against disabled people for any program that receives federal funds.

1974—Congress passes the Equal Educational Opportunities Act, which prohibits discrimination based on race, color, and national origin, and calls for school districts to take action on language barriers to education, which made bilingual education more available in schools.

1978—In University of California v. Bakke, the United States Supreme Court upholds the practice of affirmative action, but rules that racial quotas are unconstitutional.

1979—Robert "Bob" Johnson founds Black Entertainment Television (BET) and launches the BET network in 1980.

1981—President Ronald Regan appoints Sandra Day O'Connor to the United States Supreme Court. Sandra Day O'Connor is the first woman appointed to the Supreme Court.

DIVERSIFY OR DIE: DIVERSITY. INCLUSION. EVOLUTION. SUCCESS.

1982—John H. Johnson is named to Forbes list of 400 Richest Americans.

1984—Walter Mondale selects Geraldine Ferraro as the first woman vice-presidential candidate of a major political party.

1984—Oprah Winfrey launches her production company and gains international syndication for her television show that will become the most popular television show in history.

1986—Congress passes the Immigration Reform and Control Act legalizing some undocumented workers and sets forth sanctions for employers that hire illegal aliens.

1987—Reginald Lewis purchases Beatrice International Foods from Beatrice Companies for $985 million. Lewis renamed the company to TLC Beatrice International, the largest African American owned and managed business in the US, and the first black-owned company to have more than $1 billion in annual sales.

1987—Dr. Clifton R. Wharton, Jr. becomes Chairman and CEO of TIAA-CREF, distinguishing him as the first black CEO of a Fortune 500 company.

1987—The Hudson Institute publishes, "The Changing Workforce: Demographic Issues Facing the Federal Government" (commonly known as "Workforce 2000").

1989—Eastman Kodak is one of the first companies to decide to outsource its information technology systems to foreign countries (creating a whole new level of cultural diversity challenges for its US managers).

1990—Buying Power by Race:
Native Americans:	$20 Billion
Asians:	$115 Billion
Hispanics:	$210 Billion
African Americans:	$316 Billion

A MODERN SOCIO-ECONOMIC HISTORY OF DIVERSITY

1991—Diversity thought leader R. Roosevelt Thomas publishes the book, Beyond Race and Gender: *Unleashing the Power of Your Total Workforce by Managing Diversity.*

1995—The Internet is commercialized, providing a massive platform for global commerce and information exchange. This is a critical component for the advancement of diversity.

1997—The Hudson Institute publishes, "Workforce 2020—Work and Workers in the 21st Century." Workforce 2020 is a follow up to Workforce 2000.

1998—In Oncale v. Sundowner Offshore Systems, the United States Supreme Court rules same-sex sexual harassment is actionable under Title VII. The plaintiff must prove the discrimination was because of sex and that the harassment was severe.

1999—Andrea Jung took the helm of the cosmetics giant Avon as the first Asian CEO of a Fortune 500 Company.

2000—Buying Power by Race:
Native Americans: $40 Billion
Asians: $272 Billion
Hispanics: $448 Billion
African Americans: $600 Billion

2001—Bob Johnson becomes the first African American billionaire when he sells BET to Viacom.

2001—DiversityInc.com publishes the first DiversityInc Top 50 list, creating one of the most influential lists recognizing US-based companies for their diversity efforts.

2002—Telemundo is purchased by NBC for $2.7 billion.

DIVERSIFY OR DIE: DIVERSITY. INCLUSION. EVOLUTION. SUCCESS.

2003—In <u>Grutter v. Bollinger</u>, the most important affirmative action decision since the 1978 Bakke case, the United States Supreme Court (5–4) upholds the University of Michigan Law School's policy, ruling that race can be one of many factors considered by colleges when selecting their students because it furthers "a compelling interest in obtaining the educational benefits that flow from a diverse student body."

2003—New census numbers show that the Hispanic community is the largest minority group in the USA.

2008—Sen. Barack Obama, Democrat from Chicago, becomes the first African American to be nominated as a major party nominee for president of the United States.

2008—On November 4, Barack Obama becomes the first African American to be elected president of the United States.

2009—President Barack Obama nominates Sonia Maria Sotomayor to the United States Supreme Court. Sonia Maria Sotomayor is the first Latina Justice appointed to the Supreme Court.

2010—Buying Power by Race:
  Native Americans: $87 Billion
  Asians: $609 Billion
  African Americans: $947 Billion
  Hispanics: $1 Trillion

2010—MBDA and the US Census Bureau announce that the number of minority-owned firms increased by 46 percent to a total of 5.8 million between 2002 and 2007 according to data from the "Preliminary Estimates of Business Ownership by Gender, Ethnicity, Race, and Veteran Status: 2007," from the US Census Bureau's 2007 Survey of Business Owners.

A MODERN SOCIO-ECONOMIC HISTORY OF DIVERSITY

2011—President Barack Obama enacts Executive Order 13583, which establishes a coordinated government-wide initiative to promote diversity and inclusion in the workplace.

2011—Tim Cook becomes CEO at Apple. Tim Cook is the first openly gay CEO of a Fortune 500 company.

2012—Buying Power by Race:
Native Americans:	$103 Billion	156% increase since 2000
Asians:	$716 Billion	164% increase since 2000
African Americans:	$1 Trillion	73% increase since 2000
Hispanics:	$1.2 Trillion	142% increase since 2000

By comparison, there was a 60% increase in white buying power since 2000.

2013—Television networks ABC and Univision launch a new cable network called "Fusion" targeting US Hispanics.

2015—In Obergefell et al v. Hodges Director, Ohio Department of Health et al., the United States Supreme Court, in a 5–4 ruling, decided that gay marriage is legal.

Future:
2017—Buying Power by Race (projected):
Native Americans:	$148 Billion
Asians:	$1 Trillion
African Americans:	$1.3 Trillion
Hispanics:	$1.7 Trillion

Evolutionary Diversity Timeline Analysis
This timeline presents a very different viewpoint of the evolution, progression, and financial importance of diversity. This historical timeline of diversity is presented for a number of reasons:

1. The timeline starts off with Executive Orders and ends with a multi-billion dollar business deal, the appointment of diverse CEOs

of Fortune 500 companies, and a two-term African American president.
2. The timeline provides an alternate theory that diversity is still linked to affirmative action. During the forty years between 1930 and 1970, federal laws and court cases created a legal framework for affirmative action and subsequently diversity. Although there are cases, including United States Supreme Court cases, from 1990 forward to address the issue of affirmative action, the conservative Supreme Court actually decreases the role of affirmative action.
3. This timeline strongly incorporates the buying power by race to showcase the increased economic buying power of Native Americans, Asians, African Americans, and Hispanics. As a CEO, if you have not developed products, marketing plans, or diverse sales teams, are you failing to capitalize on a four trillion dollar market in 2017?

In the spirit of Darwinism, let's analyze critical components of the evolution of the old forms to the new forms to deepen the analysis of the case for diversity. The analysis will focus on the following areas: The economic leverage of the multicultural economy, outsourcing, Workforce 2000 and Workforce 2020, mergers and acquisitions, and social media.

The Economic Leverage of the Multicultural Economy
The University of Georgia, Terry College of Business, Selig Center for Economic Growth published "The Multicultural Economy 2012," an article authored by Jeffrey M. Humphreys. This article predicted that the combined buying power of African Americans, Asians, and Native Americans would account for 15.3 percent of the nation's total buying power in 2012, up from 12.5 percent in 2000, and from 10.6 percent in 1990.

The gain in combined market share of 2.8 percent from 2000 to 2012 for African-Americans, Asians and Native Americans amounts to an additional $340 billion in buying power in 2012. The market share claimed by a targeted group of consumers is important because the higher their market share, the lower the average cost of reaching a potential buyer in the group. The author also predicted the combined buying power of these three racial groups will rise to $2.5 trillion in 2017, accounting for 16.4 percent of the nation's total buying power.

These figures are important because the buying power of the diversity community is growing. As the buying power grows, the purchasing power grows. The increase in purchasing power opens the possibility to new customers with increased discretionary funds.

Outsourcing
In 1989, outsourcing, specifically offshore outsourcing, became a popular part of corporate America. Offshore outsourcing was used to increase profits by reducing labor and supplier costs. Companies contracted labor in developing countries that met the following criteria: English speaking population, low wages and cost of living, liberal labor laws, and good educational system. Countries that meet these criteria have a low cost, moderately educated workforce. One of the first companies to engage in overseas outsourcing was Eastman Kodak when they outsourced their information technology systems.

Modern day outsourcing had a huge impact on diversity. Corporations reduced the US labor side of the workforce, which had a greater impact on diverse employees. Outsourcing also presented new diversity challenges as it increased the differences in culture and communication not only between the US manager and the outsourced employee, but also the outsourced employee and the public if the position required public interface (i.e., customer service call line, IT help desk, etc.). Outsourcing required managers in the US to adapt to different cultures, languages, cultural norms, and work standards. This is where diversity training filled a troublesome void.

When coordinating and attending outsourcing diversity management training, the goal of the training was to educate the managers on the cultural differences and how to manage them. Diversity training helped bridge the management and cultural gap between the manager and international multicultural team. Once managers were educated on the cultural norms and different methods of communication, they adjusted and diversified their management style and communications to improve the multicultural managerial relationship.

DIVERSIFY OR DIE: DIVERSITY. INCLUSION. EVOLUTION. SUCCESS.

Workforce 2000

The Employment and Training Administration of the United States Department of Labor provided a grant to the Hudson Institute to conduct research on the American workforce. The result was *Workforce 2000*.

The Workforce 2000 researchers found four key trends that would shape the last years of the twentieth century:
- The American economy should grow at a relatively healthy pace, boosted by the rebound in US exports, renewed productivity growth, and a strong world economy.
- Despite its international comeback, US manufacturing would be a much smaller share in the economy in the year 2000 than it was at the time of publication. Service industries would create all of the new jobs, and most of the new wealth, over the years between *Workforce 2000's* publication and the year 2000.
- The workforce would grow more strongly, becoming older, more female, and more disadvantaged. Only 15 percent of the net new entrants to the labor force over those thirteen years would be native white males compared to 47 percent in that category at the time.
- The new jobs in service industries would demand much higher skill levels than the jobs of the time, yet very few new jobs would be created for those who cannot read, follow directions, or use mathematics. Ironically, the demographic trends in the workforce, coupled with the higher skill requirements of the economy, would lead to both higher and lower unemployment: more joblessness among the least-skilled and less among the most educationally advantaged.

Workforce 2020

In Workforce 2020, the follow up publication to *Workforce 2000*, the Hudson Institute validated the findings set forth in *Workforce 2000*:
1. As *Workforce 2000* was "misread," the authors set the record straight in *Workforce 2020*.
2. The authors analyzed new data and interpreted the data on a national and regional level.

A brief analysis follows:

A MODERN SOCIO-ECONOMIC HISTORY OF DIVERSITY

Workforce 2000 was interpreted as stating there would be a scarcity in the white male workforce. In *Workforce 2020*, the authors drew the distinction between "entrants" and "net new entrants." The net new entrants in the workforce would increasingly consist of women and minorities; thus, showing *Workforce 2000* did not predict a scarcity of white males in the workforce, but a gradual and inevitable shift based on census data. Also, *Workforce 2000* focused on national data, while *Workforce 2020* shows the importance of regional data. California, for example, already has and will continue to have larger numbers of minorities, especially Mexican-American Latinos, than other parts of the United States.

Workforce 2000 and *Workforce 2020* are important because the information in both publications proved to be correct. National, state, and local organizations should use demographic trends and patterns to evolve and adapt to their new environment. If the trends and patterns are ignored and you fail to plan, you plan to fail.

Mergers and Acquisitions in the Diversity Timeline

The historical analysis shows large companies recognize the evolution of diversity as the profit example of the twenty-first century. The proof is in the number of acquisitions and mergers of diverse companies. The diversity timeline includes four purchases, mergers or acquisitions including:

- 1987—Reginald Lewis purchases Beatrice International Foods from Beatrice Companies for $985 million. Lewis renamed the company to TLC Beatrice International; the largest African American owned and managed business in the US, and the first black-owned company to have more than $1 billion in annual sales.
- 2001—Bob Johnson becomes the first African American billionaire when he sells BET to Viacom.
- 2002—NBC purchases Telemundo for $2.7 billion.
- 2013—Television networks ABC and Univision launch a new cable network called "Fusion" targeting US Hispanics.

Reginald Lewis is different than the other mergers and acquisitions, as his minority-owned company purchased a company that had over a billion

DIVERSIFY OR DIE: DIVERSITY. INCLUSION. EVOLUTION. SUCCESS.

dollars in sales. All of the other mergers, acquisitions and joint ventures were successful and evolutionary as the purchasing companies recognized the financial reward, customer base, and brand value of the diverse company and their customer base. All of purchasing companies wisely decided to keep the brand and the active in the community. Brand value is critical as these brands had a strong, dedicated, loyal customer base. For example, changing the name from BET to another Viacom name would have dramatically reduced the value of the BET brand and most likely reduced profits as customers often leave businesses when the brand is compromised or changed.

Social Media
A common theme throughout this book is to analyze an organization's ability to evolve and diversify to a changing, perhaps hostile, business environment. The creation of the Internet and social media dramatically changed the global business environment.

At first, social media seemed like a new and harmless way to communicate and share information. Then, in 1999, a free peer-to-peer file sharing service named Napster was created. Napster drastically changed the music industry business to the point where the music industry sued Napster for copyright infringement. In the end, Napster filed Chapter 11 and was sold for 85 million, but the damage to the music industry was already done. A new business form evolved and the music, film, publishing and TV industries were faced with a major evolution they did not control.

Aside from intellectual property challenges, social media presents the opportunity for businesses to expand to every wireless and Internet connection in the world. The ability to instantly share one's thoughts, experiences, and culture through social media makes the world a much smaller space. Anyone with connection to the Internet and a device (phone, tablet, or computer) can connect, post pictures and videos, tweet, follow, share, like, and do all of the other social media activities.

Social media is also a powerful business marketing tool. Many companies use social media to market products, give surveys, find new clients, and screen new applicants. This has had a huge impact on diversity. Social media is also the perfect stage for diversity, as organizations can immediately communicate to new cultures. Unlike other forms of communication, ill-chosen words on social media can immediately reach millions, can also cost companies millions, and dramatically damage the brand.

Diversifying Social Media

Social media is the great equalizer. Most of social media is free, which provides unlimited access to anyone with Internet access. However, anything that can be used for profit can create inequality, including social media.

Diversity in the social media business is a hotly debated topic, especially in blogs. Generally, the contributors to the blogs have three different perspectives.

The first perspective is that social media is free and equal to all so diversity does not matter. The second is social media is already "diverse" as a large percentage of the diverse population uses social media. The third school of thought is that the social media ownership, finance, and management is not diverse because it is dominated by white males. All three are correct, but that does not tell the entire story.

1. Social Media is Free and Equal to All

In the first perspective, social media is a free, equal to all, and does not discriminate. A similar argument is that filing corporation papers in any state office, the 501(c)(3) not for profit application filed with the IRS, or the charter of the government agency designed to use tax payers dollars to serve their constituents are mediums to all and in and of itself does not discriminate. However, it is the action and the communication of the executives and employees that result in discrimination, not the type of business or legal structure. But don't rely on the theory of this conversation; racism, hatred, and discrimination are all openly posted about on social media sites including blogs and video sites. All the proof you need to find racism, hatred, and discrimination is on social media.

Enter the worst words of hate you can think of after a hashtag. After you find these hashtag words, then realize the people who posted these words may work next to diverse employees, or worse, supervise the same people that are the subject of their posts. In preparation for a number of presentations on the new realities of social media in employment, I researched posts, photos, and comments that resulted in the termination of employees. I could not use much of the social media content because it was so racist that I was afraid it would anger my audience and derail the presentation.

While social media is not perfect, it has provided opportunities to many that would not have otherwise been exposed to these opportunities. For example, crowdfunding has helped tens of thousands of small businesses and organizations to raise capital they would not otherwise have access to. Another example includes websites that allow people to provide micro loans to small companies in third world countries.

2. Social Media is Already Diverse
The second perspective is based on social media usage, not control or financial gain. Studies show the diverse population, specifically African Americans and Latinos, engage in greater use of Facebook and Twitter. According to a February 2015 Pew Research Center article, "Social Media Vary by Race and Ethnicity," Latinos and Blacks are more likely to use Instragram and Pinterest. The article also points out the average age of social media use is Latinos is younger than the other groups: Latinos (22), Blacks (33), and Whites (42).

The fact that diverse populations use social media does not mean that the social media industry is "diverse." When determining the diversity in social media companies, the measure should not be who is using social media but the level of diversity at all levels of the social media company. Social media companies may not have a history of discrimination because they are still relatively new to the business world. However, that is changing as the public is paying attention to the lack of diversity numbers at the highest levels of the largest social media companies.

3. Social Media Ownership
In the third perspective, social media has created multi-billion dollar businesses. Fortunes have been made based on the use of this "free" medium. Thus, whenever profit is in play, traditional issues of equality, good and bad, come into play.

CB Insights reports that less than 1% of Internet company founders are African Americans and 12% are Asian American. That figure alone shows how profit from free social media sites do not financially benefit the large parts of the diversity community. African Americans, Latinos, and Native-Americans lack the accessible capital and credit to start substantial Internet and social media companies.

The relationship between social media and diversity is just starting. Since social media has a larger grassroots component than other marketing and advertising mediums, the diversity community has greater control of the content and greater control to criticize the content, so the diversity community has more control of the outcome.

However, organizations should also recognize the nature of their social media client base and use diversity within their organization to communicate to the diversity community. Similar to the discussion about mapping the consumption chain in Chapter 2, when companies market to customers without understanding their client's culture, they may pay the price. The stakes are higher in social media as once the culturally insensitive marketing goes "viral," the company is in full-scale apology mode and damage control.

Evolve and Succeed
- Has your organization reviewed the statistics related to buying power by race for your organizational footprint?
- What are your social media marketing efforts for your diverse customers?

DIVERSIFY OR DIE: DIVERSITY. INCLUSION. EVOLUTION. SUCCESS.

- Do your social media messages address the issues of the diversity community?
- Does your organization employ diverse employees that understand the nuisances of the diversity community?

CHAPTER 5
THE EVOLUTION OF DIVERSITY AND INCLUSION BEYOND AFFIRMATIVE ACTION

"Though nature grants vast periods of time for the work of natural selection, she does not grant an indefinite period; for as all organic beings are striving, it may be said, to seize on each place in the economy of nature, if any one species does not become modified or improved in a corresponding degree with it's competitors, it will soon be exterminated."

— Charles Darwin *On The Origin of Species*

Diversity had to evolve from a compliance issue to a profitable business practice in order to adapt to the business environment and survive. If, as Charles Darwin states, diversity had not "modified or improved in a corresponding degree," diversity would be extinct. As shown in the previous chapter, diversity has moved through a complex evolutionary process. For example, at some point, "diversity" became "diversity and inclusion." However, diversity is still evolving. The complete separation of diversity from affirmative action and EEO is the next step in evolution.

The separation of affirmative action from diversity does not mean that affirmative action and EEO are no longer necessary. From a legal perspective, statistical evidence proves racial and gender equality has not been achieved.

DIVERSIFY OR DIE: DIVERSITY. INCLUSION. EVOLUTION. SUCCESS.

EEOC Charge Statistics from FY 1997 – FY 2014	
Fiscal Year	**Number of Charges**
1997	80,680
1998	79,591
1999	77,444
2000	79,896
2001	80,840
2002	84,442
2003	81,293
2004	79,432
2005	75,428
2006	75,768
2007	82,792
2008	95,402
2009	93,277
2010	99,922
2011	99,947
2012	99,412
2013	93,727
2014	88,778

As the EEOC statistics show, EEOC charges have steadily increased since 1997 and peaked in FY 2011 at 99,947. While the charges have slightly decreased in FY 2013 and 14, they are still significantly above the number of charges filed in FY 1997.

Legally, affirmative action and EEO will always play an important role. From this perspective, affirmative action is used to reduce the risk of litigation. If affirmative action employment numbers are in line with the local and regional population, then the organization has an affirmative defense to show they are sufficiently hiring and keeping diverse employees.

However, while affirmative action is a legal principle that is enforced by the US government, diversity is not a tool to reduce risk. Diversity is a profitable global business practice that is not "enforced" by government, laws, or regulations. Diversity is a tool to enhance the workforce, culture, products and services, and ultimately, the bottom line. Affirmative action was designed to remedy the historic and current injustices of slavery and discrimination. But this is just the point isn't it? Affirmative action was designed to right the wrongs of the past while diversity creates a competitive environment for the future. In short, affirmative action was the legal standard of the twentieth century; diversity is the global standard of the twenty-first century. So why can't diversity completely separate from affirmative action?

In the 1991 landmark publication, *Beyond Race and Gender*, Roosevelt Thomas argued that affirmative action was an important tool to recruit and integrate large numbers of minorities and women into the workforce, but the affirmative action approach has many flaws. Mr. Thomas argues managing diversity, not affirmative action, is the approach that can provide long lasting cultural results. Mr. Thomas states:

Managing diversity doesn't seek to give relief from a system's negative consequences by adding on supplementary efforts. Instead, it begins with taking a hard look at the system and asking the questions that were not asked: Why doesn't the system work naturally for everyone? What has to be done to allow it to do so? Will the cultural roots of this company allow us to take the necessary cultural action? If not, what root changes have to be made?

Mr. Thomas' numerous books and public speaking engagements increased the dialogue of diversity in the business environment. Where companies were using affirmative action as the primary tool to justify the hiring and retention of people of color and women, Mr. Thomas gave the businesses community a business tool to diversify and add value to the human capital of the company. Twenty-five years later, most businesses can still learn from the teachings of Mr. Thomas.

Diversity and Inclusion Should Not Replace Affirmative Action
It has been my experience that the most impactful actions for diversity only occur when the organization is facing a lawsuit, fails an Office of Federal Contract Compliance Audit, or faces other legal actions. When the employees sue their employer or the government finds a company is not in compliance,

there is a fundamental shift in power because the decisions and actions are taken from the employer and placed in the hands of a judge, government attorney or investigator, or another third party. Once the employer's power to make decisions is threatened, the employer uses an impressive amount of internal and potentially external resources to defend their power and decisions. When the employee and the employer or the government and the employer are in this power struggle, it is probably too late to engage in productive communications. Both parties have lost the opportunity to proactively work together to embrace and engage in the power of diversity.

A common perspective is to use diversity and inclusion rather than affirmative action to empower organizations to mitigate discrimination. However, affirmative action and the legal efforts to eradicate racism are still needed in the present day for legal, educational, and financial reasons. We have sufficiently discussed legal and educational aspects, but before we discuss the use of diversity to generate revenue for your organization, let's discuss the use of diversity as a cost savings tool.

A report from the Center for American Progress shows that workforce discrimination against employees based on race, gender, or sexual orientation costs employers an estimated $64 billion a year? Sixty-four billion dollars! That is a lot of money that can be used to manufacture more products, deliver more services, invest in infrastructure, develop new technologies, and make more money. As many of the workforce discrimination complaints are started by the actions of supervisors and managers; that is the first place to look to mitigate the cost and find the components in your organization that do not support diversity efforts. In line with the diversity evolution theory of Diversify or Die, employees who do not support diversity are the employees who do not support evolution of the organization.

Who are the Enemies of Evolution in Your Organization?
There are employees in every organization who do not represent the best interests of the organization. In their minds it is more important to conduct business the way they want to rather than the way they should. These employees are enemies of evolution.

THE EVOLUTION OF DIVERSITY AND INCLUSION

Everyone knows these employees, but may not recognize the negative impact they have on the organization. In the late 1990s, Hyundai and Kia were ranked as the thirteenth largest automaker in the world. Since then, Hyundai improved quality, reduced defects, installed more features, and offered a hundred-thousand-mile warranty. All of these were unheard of in the automotive industry. Hyundai drove right past Ford to become the fifth largest automaker in the world. Hyundai has a creative way of incorporating diversity into their corporate culture. In the Wall Street Journal article about Hyundai, "Once a Global Also-Ran, Hyundai Zooms Forward," the authors Mike Ramsey and Evan Ramstad report:

> *Instilling creative thinking is a work in progress. A few times a week, video screens around Hyundai's headquarters in Seoul show a one-minute clip that has become a favorite among staffers. It shows an open office where workers wearing the same shirt and haircut are beavering away. Then a new person arrives with a different haircut. Each time he voices an idea, the others shout him down. Eventually he gets the same haircut and everybody likes him. Then a question appears: "Aren't we stuck in conventional thinking?"*

Hyundai found a creative and effective way to promote diversity and defeat the enemies of evolution. Hyundai realized they had to stop conventional thinking and evolve to compete in the global automotive market. Planting the seeds of evolution in every level of the organization and making it visible on a daily basis gave Hyundai the evolutionary advantage it needed to compete and accelerate past the competition.

Midlevel Management Behaviors

Who are the actual enemies of evolution in your organization? To help you identify these employees you will find a Midlevel Management Behavior example below. Why include behavior examples? Because midlevel managers may have the mindset that conventional thinking is part of their job. Any employee can speed up an organization's path to extinction, but a manager has more power and influence to negatively impact the employees and the organization.

DIVERSIFY OR DIE: DIVERSITY. INCLUSION. EVOLUTION. SUCCESS.

Once the focus is on the manager's behavior, ideals, and actions rather than their name, face, and connections in the organization, it is much easier to identify and properly address their actions in the workplace.

Midlevel Management Behavior Example #1
The midlevel manager:
- Has a record of making inappropriate statements to employees.
- Does not adapt to change, but marginalizes it by saying, "the powers that be want us to do it this way, but we are going to do it my way instead."
- Always blames someone else for everything, especially Human Resources and Legal.
- Has a record of saying that people are not "qualified" without reading their résumé or interviewing them.
- Does not believe in diversity as a business practice.
- Does not have the qualifications for the position, but are told they will "grow in to the position," have "transferrable skills," or bring a "fresh perspective," while there are qualified applicants that can immediately serve in the midlevel management position.

Does this sound like a midlevel manager in your organization? Did a particular manager come to mind? This manager may be an enemy of evolution. In my corporate and consulting life, I have known many midlevel managers that fit that description. These managers are a huge risk to the organization and prevent the evolution of the organization. The presence of these managers creates an element of extinction that will spread in your organization.

Midlevel Management Behavior Example #2
Here, the midlevel manager:
- Is open to positive and constructive change;
- Does not unjustly blame other departments;
- Treats all employees equally and fairly; and
- Believes in diversity as a business practice.

Honestly, there are more Midlevel Management Examples that fit this scenario than fit the first Midlevel Manager; however, the first Midlevel

Manager probably exists somewhere in every organization. If Midlevel Manager #1 is managing three, five, ten, or twenty employees, their poor managerial actions have a negative multiplier effect on the organization. In other words, the more people they manage poorly, the greater the negative impact on the organization. These are the managers that create an extinction risk to the organization. It may not be in one day, or with one employee, but given time and repeat chances, the extinction risk increases.

How Can You Tell When Diversity Efforts are Working?

In many of my hybrid diversity positions, I had to analyze data on diversity metrics: hires, promotions, terminations, and increases in grade based on race, gender, disability, and veteran status.

There are always two ways to look at diversity data: raw numbers and statistical impact. For example, a statistical analysis when one African American female was promoted brought the total number in the grade band from one to two, equating to a 100% increase in promotions in African American females. While this promotion represents small progress, a more impactful statistic would be found by comparing this progress against the total number of employee promotions in the same grade band.

The objective of reviewing diversity data should be to determine where diversity efforts have succeeded, failed, and need improvement to succeed. If your organization is analyzing diversity data only to find small superficial successes to argue the current diversity approach is sufficient, then the data is not being used to add to the success of your organization; it is being used to justify failures.

The Anatomy of a Diversity Department

The diversity department is usually used to analyze diversity statistics, oversee Employee Resource Committees, create an inclusive workplace, and sometimes resolve employee issues. In many organizations, diversity employees are usually AA/compliance, human resources employees, or attorneys, especially labor and employment attorneys. The absence of formal diversity education or training, combined with the usual lack of a budget or resources, creates a situation in which the role of the diversity department is what the employee makes of it.

DIVERSIFY OR DIE: DIVERSITY. INCLUSION. EVOLUTION. SUCCESS.

Support from the CEO and Senior Executives
I have seen many examples where the CEO and senior executive say the right things when it comes to diversity, includes the right statements in the annual report and marketing materials, and say the right things in speeches. But when it comes to actions, it seems that applying diversity programs is the furthest thing from their minds. Diversity becomes a show with no script, no funding, and no stage. In order for a diversity program to make sustained business change, the CEO must adequately fund and actively support diversity efforts on a regular basis. This also helps to ensure midlevel managers are professionally embracing the concept of diversity. After all, as stated earlier in the book, employees look to the actions of their managers more than their words.

I have seen many organizations brag about successful diversity efforts, but the extent of diversity in the managerial and senior executive ranks does not come close to looking like their employees, client base, or the community. Success is in actions, not statements. The key words here are delegation, urgency, and accountability.

Delegation: Diversity Words and Diversity Actions
As a CEO, managing employees is a business necessity. Of course, the CEO's senior staff is responsible for carrying out the CEO's orders. What happens if the senior staff does not agree with the CEO's diversity orders? Usually diversity efforts fail for lack of execution. Thus, while the CEO is communicating diversity, if middle management is not following the orders of the CEO, the workforce does not see any positive diversity actions.

Diversity words without diversity actions creates a lack of trust and decreases employee moral. This is why delegation, urgency, and accountability are critical to successful application of diversity efforts.

Essentially, executives have two critical questions to ask their senior staff:
1. Do you have quantitative goals to determine the level of success of your diversity efforts?
2. Are you supporting and enforcing the efforts to attain the diversity goals?

THE EVOLUTION OF DIVERSITY AND INCLUSION

Simply creating diversity policies, practices, trainings, and departments is not evolution. A positive response to both of these questions sets the stage for evolution to occur. True evolution only occurs when the required or desired change takes effect in the entire organization.

Urgency: Do as I do, Not as I Say

Actions create more urgency than words. Actions are the first steps any executive can take in showing the urgency of diversity. The next step is to communicate the urgency to middle management. If leaders do not connect diversity and inclusion to the organization's objectives and mission statement with urgency, middle management will not have the incentive to carry out the executive leadership orders.

Accountability: No Accountability Means No Progress

Another very important factor to communicate urgency is accountability. Productivity decreases when employees are not held accountable for their performance and conduct. There are many accountability tools including performance plans, performance evaluations, goals and quotas, and measurement of time effectiveness. These tools are only effective if used to actually improve performance and productivity by holding the employee accountable if their performance fails.

If the CEO and senior leadership are serious about the diversity department and diversity programs, they will hold managers accountable just as they would for any other performance measurement. Once managers realize they are being held accountable, the delegation, urgency, and accountability combination will be complete.

Diversity Bait and Switch

The following is an example where the delegation, urgency, and accountability combination fell apart. After *Workforce 2000* was published, one company recognized the importance of diversity and decided to create long-term diversity goals based on race and gender within professional, managerial, and executive ranks. They even set a deadline to accomplish the diversity goals. Sounds great, right? Not so fast.

DIVERSIFY OR DIE: DIVERSITY. INCLUSION. EVOLUTION. SUCCESS.

As the deadline drew near, the executives realized they were not going to reach their diversity goals. So what did this company do next? They changed the rules of the game. Instead of holding managers accountable, they changed their diversity goals to a far lower standard and promoted their small successes. Even when reasonable diversity goals were created, company leaders did not hold themselves or middle management accountable for their failure to meet the diversity goals. If employers are not willing to hold themselves responsible when they do not succeed, then diversity and inclusion is all talk and no action.

Evolve and Succeed
- Analyze the actions of your managers and executives; do their actions represent the future of your organization?
- Review the Midlevel Management Behavioral Example #1. Do any managers exhibit the characteristics in that example?
- If you find Midlevel Management Behavioral Example #1 in your organization, what efforts are in place to reduce or prevent the risk of extinction?
- Is diversity linked to affirmative action or EEO in your organization?
- Is your diversity department effective while it maintains responsibility for diversity and affirmative action or EEO?

CHAPTER 6

WHERE IS YOUR DIVERSITY DEPARTMENT LOCATED IN YOUR ORGANIZATION?

"Thus, as I believe, natural selection will always succeed in the long run to reducing and saving every part of the organization, as soon as it is rendered superfluous, without by any means causing some other part to be largely developing any organ, without rejecting as a necessary compensation the reduction of some adjoining part."

— Charles Darwin *On The Origin of Species*

The diversity department is usually the center for diversity in an organization, but as any experienced diversity professional will tell you, larger is not necessarily better.

I recall when diversity was first introduced in the early 1990s. Many managers called diversity a fad or a passing business concept. I even recall one manager calling diversity a cultural food day. Over twenty years later, diversity has evolved to serve as a critical domestic and international business practice. Colleges and universities are starting to create diversity curriculum and many accredited organizations are offering certificates in diversity. So much for the diversity fad.

But diversity is not one size fits all. Like every other business practice, the concept of diversity, as well as the diversity department, must be custom designed for the benefit of organization.

DIVERSIFY OR DIE: DIVERSITY. INCLUSION. EVOLUTION. SUCCESS.

In organizations, departments have to fit in an organizational chart. So where is the best departmental location for diversity? Let's take a look at some common locations.

Human Resources

Many organizations place the diversity department in the Human Resource department (HR). A common practice is to combine EEO and affirmative action with diversity as an HR function. Sometimes the three functions are combined into one position, so the actual diversity efforts are only a percentage of the employee's responsibilities. If you are a government contractor during the hectic times of filing the required annual reports and completing affirmative action plans, your hybrid diversity employee does not have the time to focus on diversity. In another example, when the diversity practitioner has to collect data to respond to a lawsuit on short notice, diversity efforts take the back seat to the critical affirmative action and EEO issues of the day.

If you are a small organization, having one diversity professional with other HR responsibilities may be sufficient. It is important to note the argument for a well funded and adequately staffed diversity department is not to spend an unnecessary amount of time or money. Proper investment as compared to the size of the organization, workplace environment, employee base and demographics, and diversity of geographic locations is a prudent way to ensure your business is poised to evolve as the business environment changes.

If you are a medium to large organization, you should determine if you have allocated sufficient resources for diversity and inclusion efforts. Are your diversity and inclusion efforts just window dressing? Do you have a diversity professional just so you can say you practice diversity? Did your diversity professional have any experience in diversity prior to accepting the role?

The decision to place the diversity department in human resources should be based on the complexity of your organization and customer base. Smaller to midsize organizations with a highly specialized product or service may not need a large diversity department outside of human resources. Diversity efforts in larger, more complex organizations will likely have more impact on an organization if it operates outside of the HR department. This is clearly an executive decision; the important point is that it should not be assumed that the diversity department should always be placed in human resources. That assumption alone may greatly reduce the impact of the organization's diversity efforts.

Diversity Department

In some organizations, a diversity manager or director leads the diversity department. The diversity manager or director may have one administrative assistant, or a shared administrative assistant, and one program coordinator.

In this scenario, a large organization may have a dedicated diversity department but how much authority does the department have to affect organizational change? The answer to that question depends on the organization's true commitment to diversity.

In some organizations, the diversity manager or director is a figurehead. In this unfortunate situation, the organization hires a leader to fill the lead diversity position under the illusion to improve diversity in the organization. The problem is the leadership in the organization does not want any real change or evolution. I have personally seen this scenario create great frustration when the diversity leader has the desire to implement real change and improve the business, but they have not been given the tools or opportunity. In many cases, this dedicated diversity leader ends up frustrated and leaves the organization to go somewhere they can effectuate real change.

Legal Department

In some organizations, the diversity department is in the legal department where the diversity manager or director is an attorney or a legal assistant. Their primary diversity responsibilities include: tracking hires, promotions, and terminations; investigating discrimination and harassment cases; and conducting trainings for legal purposes.

If the diversity department is in legal, then the organization's purpose of diversity is to prevent lawsuits or have an affirmative defense if they are sued. In this organization, diversity is in the same category as EEO and affirmative action because it communicates that the organization does not value diversity as a tool to enhance organizational effectiveness. Employees that pay attention to diversity efforts will probably be disappointed with the legal approach.

To be fair, placing diversity in the legal department has declined over the decades; however, there are organizations that still house diversity in the legal department. Remember, legal is essentially compliance and risk mitigation. The use of diversity as a profitable business practice does not sync with compliance and risk mitigation.

Operations

In this organization, the diversity department is housed in Operations and has a direct line to senior executives and the CEO.

I have always viewed this as the most impressive and effective approach to diversity. In this organization, diversity is recognized as a business imperative by organizational actions, financial backing, and authority to impact change inside and outside of the organization. When the diversity department is in operations, it is clear that the organization does not consider diversity an HR issue or a legal requirement. Organizations can send a powerful message of evolution to every manager simply by placing the diversity department in operations or another line of business that has major business responsibilities.

Under this scenario, diversity is a seamless part of the organization and not placed somewhere based on history or where it can't have any meaningful impact. At this point you may be thinking, wait a minute, if I use this approach, it may abolish the diversity department. The correct answer is: it depends.

An effectively managed diversity department and programs need the same focus as any other department in the organization. An organization cannot just create a sales department with sales goals and expect the managers and employees to independently make the sales goals every time.

WHERE IS YOUR DIVERSITY DEPARTMENT

In order to have a profitable sales department, employees need: management, quotas, sales tools, incentives, pep talks, training, updated calling lists, updated technology, new products to compete with the competition, etc. A diversity department needs a similar continual investment; otherwise the initial investment will not reap any dividends.

Common and Costly Diversity Mistakes

The most common mistakes I have seen companies make when creating or running a diversity department include the following:

- The diversity department is not designed to address organizational needs. Some organizations use a standard version of diversity in their organization and claim the diversity efforts do not work when the diversity department does not produce the expected results. By comparison, a sales and marketing approach from a manufacturing company would not work for a financial company. In addition, many organizations have not actually determined the desired financial or organizational objectives for their diversity efforts. Standard diversity efforts will only accomplish so much; diversity efforts need to be specifically designed for each organization.

- The diversity department does not have enough money or employees. Many diversity departments have very little, if any, money for their diversity efforts. In many cases, the diversity department only has one to three employees. In some organizations, the diversity department simply reviews the hires, promotions, and terminations. If the only responsibility for the diversity department is to review employment data, the department cannot implement any real change in the organization.

- If results are not produced within a short period of time, employees in the diversity department are terminated or diversity efforts are downsized. Real diversity changes in an organization are very difficult and take time, perhaps years. Meanwhile diversity opponents complain about the diversity efforts to the point where the leadership responds by reducing diversity efforts. Even if the diversity department is producing results, a few powerful employees or executives that have the ear of the CEO or the board of directors can damage the credibility of the diversity department.

Once leadership has lost confidence in the diversity department, it will likely lose resources and the ability to implement change.

What is the Status of Diversity in Your Organization?

As you are reading this book, you are probably wondering about the status of diversity in your organization. This takes us back to the definition of diversity. What is the definition of diversity in your organization? How does it compare to the definition proposed in this book?

The business practice to increase the bottom line by capitalizing on the responsible sale and distribution of goods or services to multicultural clientele and the supportive employment of multicultural employees at all levels of the organization.

Once you have reviewed the definition, you can look at the functionality of your diversity department and how it implements the definition in the workplace.

Every department, including the diversity department, needs to be continually assessed to determine their success in using the tools made available to that department: mission, finances, staff, position in corporate structure, etc. Unfortunately, it has been my experience when executives discuss diversity and inclusion and the diversity department, the assessment is often to limit or decrease funding for the diversity department and programs.

The most common reasons I have heard from executives that have not created a diversity department follow.

1. We don't have a diversity program and we are not interested in starting one for any one of the following reasons:
    - We don't believe in the concept of diversity.
    - We have insufficient money and resources.
    - Diversity is a soft skill and there is no way to measure the impact or effectiveness.
    - All employees should be treated equally, so there is no need for diversity.
    - Diversity is not necessary with common sense management.

WHERE IS YOUR DIVERSITY DEPARTMENT

- The board of directors or the CEO has not approved the creation of a diversity department.
- The organization is currently downsizing, so it is not appropriate to fund a new department.

The bottom line is these are excuses not to start a diversity department. If a senior executive or CEO had a desire to start a department, they could find the funds and lobby for the approval to start a diversity department.

2. We are interested in starting a diversity department, but we have not for the following reasons:
   - We don't know where to start.
   - We don't have the money to start a new department.
   - We don't have the resources internally to staff a diversity department.
   - We don't have executive or board support to start a diversity department.
   - We are concerned about what the employees will say if we start a diversity department.

3. We have a diversity department, but it does not do more for the following reasons:
   - The diversity department is staffed with people that do not have any experience in diversity.
   - We don't want to be criticized for putting too much company money and resources into a diversity department.
   - It only recognizes the months of celebration associated with diversity and inclusion: AA, Latino, LGBT, Asian, etc.
   - Our Employee Resource Group(s) don't meet very often, and they do not have any executive guidance, support, or input.
   - The diversity department improved diversity in the lower ranks, but not in the managerial ranks.
   - Diversity is important, but we do not feel that the diversity belongs in leadership.

The existence of a diversity department does not mean that the department is adding diversity to the business model for the organization. Don't forget, the definition of diversity for this book includes the following clause: "the

DIVERSIFY OR DIE: DIVERSITY. INCLUSION. EVOLUTION. SUCCESS.

business practice used to capitalize on the responsible sale and distribution of goods and services to multicultural clientele." Does your diversity department serve that purpose? Here are some questions to help focus on the functionality and purpose of the diversity department:
- Where is the department housed? Is it in HR?
- How is it staffed? Experienced diversity professionals?
- Is the diversity department adequately funded?
- Does the diversity department work with other departments on critical organizational objectives?
- Does the diversity department have access to the CEO?

The Critical Diversity Component: Middle Management

Middle management is the critical component for the success of diversity efforts. If middle management is not actively involved in diversity efforts, their absence will dramatically decrease the advancement of diversity in the organization as well as the actual evolution of the business. Why is middle management so critical to diversity?

Once the CEO, president, or board of directors implements diversity policies or programs, middle management has an important role in the process—managing daily diversity efforts. In the regular course of business, middle management hires, communicates and manages, promotes, disciplines, and terminates the a large percentage of employees in an organization. However, simply creating a diversity effort or policy and requiring middle management to implement the policies has many challenges. The creation or expansion of a diversity policy, practice, or department may present a different points of view than the current organizational culture. This point takes us back to the earlier discussion about protecting power and keeping the status quo. This challenge can make the practice of diversity very difficult and take a long time to take effect in an organization.

Diversity Training for Middle Managers

Diversity training is a critical component of the evolution of diversity in every organization. Middle managers have to be properly and continually trained to manage diversity in the workplace, just as they have to be properly and continually trained for their position or profession. Diversity training has become a staple in most large organizations and Fortune 500 companies.

However, is diversity training effective? That is a hotly debated topic.

In a 2012 article by the Harvard Business Review, "Diversity Training Doesn't Work," the author argues there are two reasons to provide diversity training—prevent lawsuits and create an inclusive environment. Historically, both are true. But the argument takes a wrong turn when the author states, "diversity training does not extinguish prejudice, it promotes it."

The author argues the solution is to use "communications training" rather than "diversity training" and focus on individuals communicating to individuals, not on diversity issues. While communications is an important element in diversity, changing diversity training to communications training ignores the many evolutionary benefits diversity training provides to organizations. For example, communications training does not recognize the marketing of products or services to the diversity community.

As reported in a 2008 Washington Post article "Most Diversity Training Ineffective, Study Finds," companies spend between $200,000 and $300,000 on diversity training every year. The article also found that mandatory diversity trainings conducted to avoid discrimination lawsuits were ineffective. I agree with this assessment, but not in the same perspective from the author.

Diversity training that is primarily affirmative action and EEO by content does not train on the issues of diversity for the organization. In addition, when diversity, affirmative action, and EEO are combined into one training event, the manager is not learning to use diversity as a tool to manage employees; they are learning how to reduce risk. This analysis supports the argument to uncouple diversity from affirmative action and EEO, but the argument does not end there.

Both articles point out the fact that there are numerous issues with diversity training. A review of the definition of diversity is necessary to evolve the concept of diversity training.

DIVERSIFY OR DIE: DIVERSITY. INCLUSION. EVOLUTION. SUCCESS.

The business practice to increase the bottom line by capitalizing on the responsible sale and distribution of goods or services to multicultural clientele and the supportive employment of multicultural employees at all levels of the organization.

The Evolution of Diversity Training

The lack of a definition of diversity also impacts diversity training. If diversity training does not communicate a consistent definition of diversity that specifically applies to the organization, the diversity training loses effectiveness before the training even starts. Once again, a review of the diversity equation is warranted.

Cultural identities + substantial relevance to the organization + impact on organizational effectiveness = definition of diversity.

Diversity training adds value to an organization when the training addresses all three components of the diversity equation. That means the diversity has to be specifically designed for the organization and address the objectives of the organization. Many diversity trainings only address the "cultural identities" component of the equation. However, diversity trainers are not entirely to blame for standardized diversity training products. In many cases, diversity trainers are simply responding to requests for training.

On many occasions, diversity departments have limited funds and a limited time to train certain departments or the entire staff. In this case the most common option is to request standardized diversity training to report they satisfied the diversity training requirement to the executive leadership. Any training in any topic that is not specifically designed for the profession or the organization and designed to simply say it was completed will be ineffective.

Substantial Relevance to the Organization

In addressing the "substantial relevance to the organization," the second component of the equation, diversity training must be directly linked to the objectives and mission of the organization. Generic training has less of an impact on the organization. Diversity training needs to be directly linked to the organizational culture, business needs and objectives, recruitment and retention challenges, diversity councils, and employee resource groups. Of course, a custom designed training requires additional funds and resources to match the business needs. However, diversity training fully engages all employees, managers, and executives if it includes the activities, objectives, and challenges of the organization.

In addressing the critical third component of the equation, "impact on organizational effectiveness," diversity training should directly link the organization's sale and distribution of goods or services to the diversity community and the bottom line. Diversity training should also directly link the recruitment and retention of multicultural employees to the bottom line. Effective diversity training can incorporate diversity statistics and measurements in the industry or sector to directly compare the organization's diversity efforts to the efforts of their industry. After all, competition may result in evolution. But training and diversity measurements should not end there.

A critical factor of the third component is the inclusion and analysis of diversity metrics. Diversity metrics must be included in the diversity training and organization objectives, and after the training is complete, they must be used to calculate the return on investment of the diversity training. Once the return on investment has been calculated, the diversity training can be refined to continue to support the mission of the organization.

Diversity Training Follow Up
The final component connecting diversity training to "the impact on organizational effectiveness" is there is usually no follow up after the training and diversity skills learned are rarely, if ever, used by the participants.

Diversity learning should not stop at the end of the instruction. Follow up is very important. The diversity department needs to design post-training exercises to ensure the continued use of the diversity learning. With the use of technology, this does not have to be an expensive or complicated endeavor. This follow-up approach will also demonstrate to the participants that diversity is a long-term learning process that is directly linked to the success of the organization, not a one-day exercise that is checked off and forgotten at the end of the lesson. These changes in diversity training will add value to the organization.

Diversity Policies

Diversity policies are critical to establish and maintain an effective diversity program and department. However, many diversity policies are very generic and echo the language in affirmative action and EEO laws. Diversity policies that do not make the business case specific to the organization reduce the effectiveness of diversity efforts in the organization.

Another factor for consideration is middle management's use of the diversity policies and programs. Unlike other business policies and programs, middle management is allowed to manage themselves. The controversial nature of diversity combined with the frequent failure to quantify and enforce diversity policies and programs usually end up with an insufficient structure for diversity programs. Let's look at the diversity equation again.

Cultural identities + substantial relevance to the organization + impact on organizational effectiveness = definition of diversity.

The "cultural identities" section of the equation is common in diversity policies. However, most policies do not contain sufficient "substantial relevance to the organization" or make the case for "impact on organizational effectiveness." A diversity policy with clear "substantial relevance to the organization" shows the business necessity between diversity and the organizational goals.

Whenever I am consulted to draft a diversity plan or policies, in addition to the diversity data and documentation, I request the following organizational documentation: mission statement, vision statement, organizational objectives, recent annual reports, marketing plans, and any other critical organizational documentation. These documents provide important information to improve the diversity policies and plans beyond affirmative action and EEO.

Once the "substantial relevance to the organization" is included in the diversity policy, the next step is to include "impact on organizational effectiveness." The measurable impact of diversity on the organization completes the analysis of diversity in the business case. As policy documentation usually includes high-level information, the impact on organizational effectiveness in the policy should be general. For example, specific figures, goals, and statistics should be in the diversity plan, not the diversity policy.

Evolution is not Immediate
Time is the great equalizer. The speed of evolution depends on the type of business and industry, but time is always a major factor. Organizations that do not to evolve in time may face extinction. Evolution, including diversity evolution, is an ongoing process. Organizations do not flip "diversity switches" and become diverse, it takes work, effort, commitment, and regular communications.

After I conduct a diversity training session for managers and supervisors, at least one manager comes to me after the training and says, "I thought you were going to teach me how to be diverse right now." I have also heard the following question on a regular basis: "I am having a diversity problem with an employee, how can I fix it now?" My most common response is, "Diversity is a process. As a manager, properly managing diversity has to evolve over time. You first have to accept that managing diversity is important to your department and organization, and that it is an ongoing process. By completing this training you have taken the first step; the question is, what are your second and third steps?"

This is usually not what the participant wants to hear, but it is what they need to hear. Once the training participant faces that reality, they understand diversity is a process that takes work that cannot occur in one day of training. The question they are left with is, are they willing to work to evolve?

Marketing to Diverse Customers
When I talk with executives and business owners about using diversity to obtain new clientele and customers, they usually expect diverse customers to buy their products and services overnight. When I ask them how long it takes to close new customer on a cold call the usual response is months, or years depending on the product or service. My response is to use the same

time frame for the diversity community. Asking the diversity community to buy your products and services takes the same time, effort, and resources. Anything less probably won't work.

Evolve and Succeed
- What are your funding levels for diversity in your organization? Are they similar to the rest of the funding for other departments?
- What are the staffing levels in the diversity department in your organization? How are the staffing levels compared to other departments?
- Is the diversity department led by a qualified senior employee?
- Does the organization's diversity training directly link to the organizational mission statement and objectives?
- Do your diversity policies contain substantial relevance to the organization?
- Do your diversity policies show the impact on organizational effectiveness?

CHAPTER 7

POWERFUL TOOLS FOR EVOLUTION: THE EMPLOYEE RESOURCE COMMITTEES AND DIVERSITY COUNCILS

"The imagination is one of the highest prerogatives of man. By this faculty he unites former images and ideas, independent of the will, and creates brilliant and novel results. The value of the products of our imagination depends of course on the number, accuracy, and clearness of our impressions, on our judgment and taste in selecting or rejecting the involuntary combinations, and to a certain extent on our power of voluntarily combining them."

— Charles Darwin *The Descent of Man*

The collective imagination and dedication of Employee Resource Committees, or Employee Affinity Groups, can be used to produce brilliant and novel results. In adapting Darwin's quote to the functionality of the Employee Resource Committee (ERC), the value of the ERC depends on the number of ERC participants and the accuracy and clarity of the mission, objectives, and leadership of the ERC.

ERC Lessons Learned

Historically, ERCs were created to give employees of a similar race, ethnic, or cultural background the ability to meet, network, mentor each other, and improve themselves and their workplace. Unfortunately, ERCs do not always work that way.

I recall my first ERC meeting in the 1990s. I attended as the Human Resources Consultant to the ERC. As it was the African American ERC, I was also personally interested in the ERC issues. After I was introduced to the ERC membership, the only agenda item the ERC members discussed was the cultural food day in the cafeteria where each member would bring in a few dishes to expose the other employees to African American culture.

DIVERSIFY OR DIE: DIVERSITY. INCLUSION. EVOLUTION. SUCCESS.

I was shocked this was the only agenda item for the ERC.

After a few months of attending the ERC, we started to talk about Black History Month. But every time an ERC member tried to raise a work related issue, the ERC Executive stopped the discussion before it could even start. Discouraged, employees eventually stopped attending the ERC meetings. The ERC members took matters into their own hands and started to meet on their own. When this happened, the vast majority of the employees stopped attending the official ERC.

The unapproved ERC meetings started out positive, but quickly became negative and frustrating because no one had the authority to make any changes. The unapproved ERC meetings started because the official ERC was ineffective and the employees could not leave the prior ERC experience behind. The ERC was reduced from a company supported ERC to a series of meetings were employees raised their concerns about managerial actions.

Is Your ERC a Group that Meets to Complain about Management?

One of the greatest concerns I hear from executives is that ERCs are meetings for unhappy employees to meet, complain, compare notes, and create an action plan to file a lawsuit. ERCs that focus on workplace concerns are the exception not the norm; and if the ERC is not managed properly, the organization must shoulder a great deal of the blame. It has been my experience that an ERC with a solid mission, measurable objectives, and a thoughtful and experienced leader will produce impressive results for an organization.

Let's look at two ERC scenarios:

ERC Scenario 1: A vice-president informs you as CEO that a group of employees from the same race and ethnic background want to form an ERC. As CEO, your first thought is to deny the request because you are concerned that a group of employees will only serve to air grievances and create problems. Based on your concerns you deny the request citing busy schedules, upcoming business deals, and a lack of available resources to support the ERC.

ERC Scenario 2: As the result of a similar request, you realize this is a "hot potato," so as CEO you agree to the ERC but do not create a strategy to govern, direct, or support the ERC. The ERC meets monthly, but it has minimum executive guidance, no mission or charter, and no goals to measure success. As a result, the ERC does not produce any advice or direction that adds value to the business.

Now let's approach both scenarios from the employee's perspective. In Scenario 1, the employees who requested the ERC are told that the CEO denied their request citing busy schedules, upcoming business deals, and a lack of available resources to support the ERC." However, the employees are aware of the company softball league, expensive weeklong boondoggle events twice a year, and executives that have extended lunches at least once a week.

In Scenario 2, the employees are meeting on a regular basis but they do not have any direction, goals, or objectives. As a result, employees meet to network and discuss issues in the workplace. These meetings do not produce any business value to the organization.

These very real ERC scenarios create problems for the organization. In both scenarios, the employees will be unhappy and morale will probably decrease. In the second scenario, the employee morale will probably increase when the ERC is formed and they start meeting, but the attendance and morale will probable decrease when the ERC is not able to make any changes in the organization. How can the organization benefit from an effective well-managed ERC?

The New Role of the ERC—The Evolutionary Resource Committee

Time to evolve the ERC conversation. ERCs are currently viewed as affinity groups, but what if ERCs are viewed as "think tanks," or a resource to benefit the organization by creating new ideas, products, or services? Organizations spend tens of millions of dollars on consultants, advisors, and contractors for new ideas and ways to improve existing services, why not use an existing internal resource? ERCs can benefit the organization in the following ways:

DIVERSIFY OR DIE: DIVERSITY. INCLUSION. EVOLUTION. SUCCESS.

1. ERCs can address gaps between the organization's current offerings and the needs of the diversity community. ERC members are probably customers or clients as well. If ERC members are not clients, then they likely know the clients of the organization. This means members of the ERC have outside knowledge about the organization's products, services, sales, customer service reputation, or general reputation in their community.
2. ERCs can provide marketing ideas for the diversity community. As employees and customers, ERCs provide a unique perspective of products and services for their community.
3. ERCs can be used to improve recruiting and retention efforts. ERC members may have access to qualified talent through their networks or know the best places to find talent in local communities. This access to the community saves the organization time and money in the recruiting process. ERCs also know why employees stay and leave the organization. ERC members may have important information to share about the workplace culture and environment. This is another ERC resource that should not be overlooked.

Measuring diversity is a common theme in this book. ERC programs should be tracked and measured to determine the success of each ERC. Once an ERC has leadership, a mission, objectives and goals, the ERC should partner with the leadership to create measurements to determine success.

Actual Employee Resource Group (ERG) Stories

ERGs have evolved into groups that drive business in a number of organizations. The article "Employees that Drive Business," by Jennifer Brown Consulting gives numerous examples of ERGs that helped improve the bottom line:

> *Over the last ten years, Ford's ERGs have helped sell vehicles through the company's Friends and Neighbors program. ERG members have assisted with the development and execution of marketing campaigns to diverse customers. Ride and Drives are a popular venue where ERGs solicit popular feedback about products, which they then report back to Ford engineers and designers. There is tremendous feedback*

POWERFUL TOOLS FOR EVOLUTION

in securing customer preferences about Ford's vehicles directly from diverse markets that the company is hoping to serve, and there is no company asset better equipped to perform this task than their ERGs. Ford's Asian, Indian, Chinese, Hispanic, and African American ERGs have taken advantage of these opportunities to encourage sales. They play a critical role in building customer intimacy and maintaining a strong corporate brand reputation.

The ERG examples also apply to small ticket items. Macy's was smart enough to ask their Hispanic ERG for help when they were having challenges reaching Hispanic markets.

Responding to the multi-marketing team's call for help in reaching the Hispanic market, Macy's ERG developed an electronic gift card specifically designed for this audience. The group also created a system for tracking down Return on Investment (ROI) in efforts to reach the rapidly growing marketplace.

Macy's offers a vast assortment of electronic gift cards for different occasions. The Hispanic ERG focused on creating a specialty card for Quinceañera, a hallmark celebration in the Hispanic community of a girl's 15th birthday. The ERG worked with Macy's multicultural marketing team to design the card and create Quinceañera materials to educate store managers and associates. They determined the highest Hispanic-populated stores and focused efforts there. In the first year, the Quinceañera gift card was introduced in 38 stores and contributed over US $250,000 in sales.

This is another excellent example of the power and value of the ERG.

The following are recommendations for how ERGs can provide measurable input and advice.

Diversity Sales and Marketing Measurement #1—Understand Your Cultural Audience

You decide to market and sell to the diversity community. An ERC can provide answers to the following:
- What are the spending habits of the diversity community?
- What are the general diversity numbers in your region or target audience?
- What is the discretionary income of your target audience? Have your competitors attempted to market to your targeted diversity community?
- What are your language advantages or challenges?

Once you have a better understanding of your potential customers, you can design and apply a more informed sales and marketing plan. Once you have the diversity sales and marketing data and plan, you can determine the appropriate amount of money to spend, and measure your performance based on the market research.

Diversity Sales and Marketing Measurement #2—Diversity Within Race and Culture

Sales and marketing plans are not "one size fits all." If that is your sales approach, you are probably losing sales everyday. It is said, "the riches are in the niches." The big question is, how do you successfully sell to the niches?

There are many pockets of diversity within the same race, gender, nationality, or sexual orientation. Of course, there is a balancing act, because if you slice pieces of the diversity pie too thin, your slice will be too small for any real sales and marketing. Products or services have to be balanced with your marketing and sales budget and the size of the diversity pie. The ERG can help find this balance.

Diversity Sales and Marketing Measurement #3—The Diversity Cost/Benefit Analysis

As the cost/benefit analysis is a fundamental business analysis, it should also be used in the context of diversity and inclusion. The cost of any

POWERFUL TOOLS FOR EVOLUTION

diversity program should be weighed against the benefits the diversity practices provide to the company. Of course there are types of diversity efforts that cannot be measured such as mentorship, volunteering, goodwill, and community relations. But the good news is the ERC is a wonderful, cost effective tool because the employees are volunteers and the ERC usually requires a small budget, if any.

Diversity Sales and Marketing Measurement #4 —Closing Conversion

Your diversity measurement should also analyze the sales that close compared to the sales that do not close. For example, which geographic areas, cultural pockets, and social media campaigns tend to yield more closed deals? Once the closing conversion has been identified, you can shift the resources to the more profitable pockets or re-design the sales and marketing campaign to potentially increase profitability in a less profitable area. The ERC can help with this as well because they know the geographic areas, cultural pockets, and social media.

Diversity Councils

Another powerful employee based group is the diversity council. A diversity council is a group of employees, usually including senior leaders and executives, who are chosen, or volunteer, to act as a group to further the diversity and inclusion mission and programs. This may sound like an ERC, but diversity councils differ from ERCs in many ways.

Diversity councils:
- Usually have employees from different races, cultures, ethnicities, genders, and sexual orientations.
- Have assigned members, unlike ERC membership, which is usually voluntary.
- Serve as advisory committees to the strategic diversity goals of the organization.
- Are more likely to use outside contractors than ERCs.
- May have one or more executives serving as a member of the diversity council rather than one executive liaison.
- May have the CEO serve as the leader of the diversity council.

DIVERSIFY OR DIE: DIVERSITY. INCLUSION. EVOLUTION. SUCCESS.

Diversity councils should also use the diversity equation and the organization's definition of diversity for guidance in creating goals to coordinate diversity actions. How can diversity councils add value to an organization?

If managed correctly, diversity councils can connect the operations of the organization to the diversity efforts and practices. This connection establishes diversity as a business tool to improve bottom line rather than solely housing diversity in human resources or legal.

Diversity councils also place the responsibility of applying diversity actions and policy on leadership rather than human resources or legal. In my service on diversity councils, I personally experienced leaders and executives sharing diversity successes and challenges across business lines. These peer-to-peer diversity best practice conversations added a great deal of value since they were not communicated as a compliance requirement from human resources or legal.

During these peer-to-peer conversations, managers used diversity to address improvements in operations, employee performance, and the bottom line. These conversations also identified opportunities for strategic follow up by the diversity practitioner, as the operations manager is now more receptive to diversity and inclusion after the peer conversation.

I have also seen diversity councils fail because of ineffective diversity council leadership, lack of support from managers and supervisors, failure to focus on long-term business goals, and poor selection of members for the diversity council. A discussion about each category follows.

Diversity Council Leadership

The choice for leadership of a diversity council is very important. Diversity council leaders are not only leading the council, but are also leaders for diversity in the organization. The diversity council leaders must believe in the concept of workforce diversity and the importance of applying diversity and inclusion at every level of the organization, or the diversity council will be ineffective.

I have personally seen more than one diversity council led by an ineffective leader or someone who did not use diversity as a business practice. In the worst-case scenario, both negative factors were present. In one diversity council, the leader stated on numerous occasions, "I don't know why we are here, this belongs in HR or legal." Those statements did not provide the leadership the diversity council needed to succeed. Despite complaints, the organization did not change the diversity council leadership because the organization felt he needed to be given a chance to succeed. The council accomplished very little under his leadership.

Support from Managers and Supervisors

Serving on a diversity council means the employee will have to take some time out of their duties to serve on the council. This is one of the main reasons employees choose not to serve on diversity councils, or their request to serve on the diversity council is denied. If an employee is selected to serve on a diversity council, they should be given the time to serve on the diversity council. There are many examples where employees are eager to attend and add value to diversity council meetings, but their supervisor would not support them taking time away from work.

Since this book focuses on the diversity performance measures, it is important to note that employees who serve on diversity committees should be performing at or above expected levels. The employees should know their job so well that they can make up the work time spent serving on the diversity council.

Focus on Long-term Business Goals

If diversity councils are connected to the long-term goals of the organization, the diversity council should have similar long-term business measurements and goals. As discussed many times in this book, measurements are critical to determine the success of diversity councils. Once long-term goals and metrics have been set for the diversity council, the council's success can be accurately, rather than anecdotally, measured. Of course, the diversity council should partner with the diversity department, or human resources if applicable, to make sure they have support and access to data for their diversity actions.

DIVERSIFY OR DIE: DIVERSITY. INCLUSION. EVOLUTION. SUCCESS.

Selection of Members for the Diversity Council

An effective diversity council requires a diverse membership. In this context, "diverse" also considers business line, rank in the organization, area of expertise, and location. A diversity council that only consists of employees in the same departments, positions, pay grades, or with similar years of service reduces the effectiveness of the diversity council.

Diversity councils should not be limited to the corporate office. Large organizations with many locations in different regions may have diversity issues specific to that region or location. A corporate diversity council may not address the problems in regional and local offices, so local diversity councils may be structured to report to the corporate diversity council, thereby addressing the strategic diversity on a corporate and local level.

Evolution of Employee Resource Committees and Diversity Councils

The diversity equation and definition of diversity add more value to the organization by providing guidance and consistency to ERCs and diversity councils. Use these groups to empower the ERC and diversity council to evolve. Organizations the limit the ERC or diversity council to recruiting, retention, or employee engagement and limiting the evolutionary impact the both groups can have on the organization.

Evolve and Succeed:
- Create a scorecard to link diversity to the bottom line. It is important to note that to effectively link diversity efforts to the bottom line, you have to properly fund the diversity efforts and give the diversity efforts time to take hold.
- Actively review your customer data to determine your progress in the diversity community.
- Let the environment tell you how to adapt to profit from the environment. The success of your products or services will greatly depend on the needs of the diversity community. Customization of your products or services to the needs of your clients will improve your chances of increasing sales and profits.

POWERFUL TOOLS FOR EVOLUTION

- Form the ERC as a diversity think tank to use their knowledge of the organization, products or services, and cultural identity to improve the products and services to targeted communities.
- Track the effectiveness of the ERC to measure successes and determine areas of required improvement.
- Use the ERC executive position as a tool to groom executives in need of exposure to diversity and inclusion. Also track the effectiveness of the ERC executive to determine successes and required improvement.

CHAPTER 8
DIVERSITY METRICS AND MEASUREMENT OF EVOLUTION

"It may metaphorically be said that natural selection is a daily and hourly scrutinizing, throughout the world, every variation, even the slightest; rejecting that which is bad, preserving and adding up all that is good; silently and insensibly working, whenever and wherever opportunity offers, at the improvement of each organic being in relation to its organic and inorganic conditions of life. We see nothing of these slow changes in progress, until the hand of time has marked long lapse of ages, and then so imperfect is our view into long past geological ages, that we only see that the forms of life are now different from what they formerly were."

— Charles Darwin *The Descent of Man*

Diversity programs should be constantly scrutinized to determine opportunities for improvement. Similar to Darwin's philosophy, natural selection should reject bad diversity programs and preserve and add up the good diversity efforts. In order to preserve or reject the right diversity programs, they have to be measured.

You Cannot Manage Diversity Unless You Measure Diversity

During an offsite teambuilding meeting, as a diversity exercise, we were divided into groups by race and gender and given thirty minutes to address diversity issues from that viewpoint. When the group exercise was over, the next step was to present our findings to all of the teams. This was the part of the exercise that would forever change my viewpoint of diversity measurement.

When the white men reported their discussion about measuring diversity, they asked, "why does it have to always be about numbers?" I was shocked! The men in this group were human resource employees and valued co-workers. I respected these men and spent time with them outside of the office. How could they ask that question?

DIVERSITY METRICS AND MEASUREMENT OF EVOLUTION

Knowing them as I did, I quickly came to realize they were not talking from a place of discrimination, but a place of misunderstanding. That discussion led me to wonder; if this was the viewpoint of "enlightened" men who supported diversity programs, what was the viewpoint of managers who were against measuring diversity programs? Not good.

Measuring diversity within the organization is a common theme in this book. Meaningful changes in diversity, as Darwin says, are usually "slow changes in progress." These slow changes take time—what Darwin describes as "long lapses of ages." That is where measurement and accountability are important tools to gauge the effectiveness of diversity efforts. When diversity programs are given the proper time to succeed, it is important to measure the step-by-step successes and failures of that diversity program.

Key Performance Indicators

One established business method used to measure and quantify the effects of business success is the key performance indicator. The definition of key performance indicators is fairly consistent. Kipfolio defines a key performance indicator as:

> *A measurable value that demonstrates how effectively a company is achieving key business objectives. Organizations use KPIs at multiple levels to evaluate their success at reaching targets. High-level KPIs may focus on the overall performance of the enterprise, while low-level KPIs may focus on processes in departments such as sales, marketing, or a call center.*

How do KPIs apply to diversity? Similar to sales, marketing, and other business practices, diversity is a business tool that can be measured for the return on investment once the proper key performance indicators are in place.

The first step is to choose KPIs that directly connect the organizational definition of diversity and inclusion with the organizational goals. If they are not connected, the KPIs will not work. Once the KPIs connect diversity and inclusion efforts with the organizational goals, the next step is to analyze the effectiveness of each KPI.

DIVERSIFY OR DIE: DIVERSITY. INCLUSION. EVOLUTION. SUCCESS.

There are many publications and services that sell KPI lists. These KPI lists break down the KPI by category, and when used, the organization can choose any number of KPIs that relate to their organization. At first, my intention was to provide an extensive list of KPIs that relate to diversity and inclusion; however, after careful consideration, the most beneficial path for the organization is to conduct an individual analysis for KPIs.

A useful tool to analyze KPIs is the SMART method:
>   **S**—Specific (clearly specify the intended outcome/s)
>   **M**—Measurable (quantifiable; stating exactly what the criteria for success are and how they will be assessed/measured)
>   **A**—Attainable (challenging but achievable; employee has the skills, time, resources, and authority to deliver the expected results)
>   **R**—Realistic (relevant to the employee's role; is willing and able to work toward its achievement)
>   **T**—Time-bound (clearly defined time frame or target date)

The SMART method can be refined to specifically address issues of diversity and inclusion:
>   **S**—Specific

>   Historically, the vast majority of KPIs for diversity and inclusion are based on recruiting/hires, retention, promotions, and termination. For example, Volvo publicly stated the following KPIs:
>   • Percentage of women and men among employees in the Volvo Group
>   • Percentage of women and men among managers in the Volvo Group

>   There is an additional measure related to the percentage of females in key positions, and those identified as high potentials and potentials. A measure of the different nationalities and ages of those represented in these groups is also included in this KPI.

>   In my roles in diversity and inclusion, the only KPIs were hires, retention, promotion, and termination. However, after consulting and engaging in research on diversity and inclusion, it became

DIVERSITY METRICS AND MEASUREMENT OF EVOLUTION

very apparent that setting forth KPIs as hires, retention, promotion, and termination is too broad and does not give enough detail for informed improvements. KPIs can be improved by creating short-term goals that serve as measurements to determine the success, challenges, and failures in achieving long-term goals.

KPI—Recruiting/Hires

The KPI "hires" can be far more valuable as a short-term goal. For example, sub-KPIs for the hiring process can include:

- Local and regional demographics
- Placement of job advertisements
- Number of applicants
- Number of first interviews
- Results of first interviews
- Number of second interviews
- Results of second interviews
- Number of offers
- Number of acceptances
- Number of rejections
- Reasons for rejections
- Number of hires

The sub-KPI data is more relevant and allows the employer to analyze the successes and failures and determine steps for improvement if necessary.

M—Measurable

As stated many times in this book, including the "impact on organizational effectiveness" in the diversity equation, diversity efforts should be measurable. You cannot manage diversity if you cannot measure diversity. Measurement is a key component of the KPI analysis and diversity. If properly planned, implemented, and measured, diversity efforts can clearly show the effects of diversity on the organization.

A—Attainable

DIVERSIFY OR DIE: DIVERSITY. INCLUSION. EVOLUTION. SUCCESS.

Building off of the specific and measurable components of the SMART analysis, diversity efforts must be attainable. The attainable component of SMART analysis does not only include a numerical goal, it also includes an attainable timeframe and resources to attain the goal. Unfunded or underfunded diversity efforts greatly reduce any reasonable level of attainability. If high expectations are set or ambitious diversity goals are communicated, and neither is supported by reasonable timeframes and adequate resources, diversity efforts are in jeopardy before they even commence.

R—Realistic

The realistic component of the SMART analysis is comparable to the attainable component, but in relation to diversity there is one considerable difference. Earlier in the book, I referenced the hybrid diversity positions that include EEO and affirmative action. It may not be realistic for an organization to expect the progression of major diversity efforts when one employee is performing multiple disciplines. Of course, this depends on the size and complexity of the organization. In addition, organizations should consider that an employee with the skill set to perform EEO/AA tasks might not have the same skill set to perform diversity efforts. One resource an organization can use to determine the effectiveness of combining all three into the hybrid position is the organization's diversity equation.

If the diversity equation does not have any EEO or affirmative action references, then the diversity efforts do not have any connection to EEO or affirmative action, and the job duties should be separated into different functions for the organization.

T—Time Bound

Finally, building off all other components of the SMART analysis, specific, measurable, attainable, and realistic periods of time should be established to achieve diversity efforts. In any project, if the time period for success is unattainable, the project has a low probability of success.

When I consult on diversity efforts, I like to use a phrase I learned early in

DIVERSITY METRICS AND MEASUREMENT OF EVOLUTION

my legal career. If I am faced with a project that seems unrealistic, I ask the question: "Do you want it cheap, thorough, or fast? You can have two out of three, but you can't have all three." For example, if the choice is thorough and fast, it won't be cheap. It can be cheap and thorough, but it won't be fast. Finally, it can be cheap and fast, but it won't be thorough. Time is a major factor in all of these options and it is a major factor in diversity efforts as well.

If diversity efforts are not well planned and an issue arises that requires a swift diversity response, then the diversity efforts will not be as effective. Planned diversity efforts with adequate time for successful completion is the best way to ensure success.

The KPIs for My Recruiting Program

The revised recruiting program at diversity recruiting conferences I mentioned earlier in the book, meets all of the SMART criteria.

- **Specific**—The revised recruiting program was specific as it directly related to the diversity conferences we sponsored and attended.
- **Measurable**—The number of applicants, interviews, offers, and acceptances from previous conferences did not support the sponsorship investment. The new recruiting approach showed immediate improvement in applicants, interviews, and acceptances. In addition, recruiting data showed the cost of recruiting one person to a position and showed the cost savings of the new recruiting effort.
- **Attainable**—When granted an extension to maintain sponsorship levels for one year, I did not make any promises I could not keep. One year was enough time to develop and implement an action plan. The goals were very attainable.
- **Realistic**—Fortunately, executives did not set unrealistic goals. This is an important point because many diversity practitioners can tell you they are often given unrealistic goals with little resources and short time frames. In an unrealistic environment, success is unlikely.

- **Time bound**—As the time frame was one year, the KPI was time bound.

"Substantial Relevance" in the Diversity Equation

In addition to the SMART analysis, "substantial relevance" is an important part of an effective KPI analysis. The components of the diversity equation are critical to determining substantial relevance. As substantial relevance is very different based on industries and companies, this book does not provide a list of substantially relevant categories.

The Time Factor in Diversity Metrics and Measurement

The second part of Darwin's quote addresses the time factor in evolution: "we see nothing of these slow changes in progress until the hands of time have marked long lapses of ages." It has been stated many times in this book that diversity is a controversial topic that can take many years to create change. One of the critical considerations when setting diversity measurements is to set a sufficient time frame to measure the results of diversity programs.

Diversity measurements can offer much more than human resources statistics. If compiled properly, diversity measurements can also gauge the impact of diversity on profitability. One of the best benchmarks for publicly traded companies is stock performance.

Long-Term Diversity Stock Analysis

In a stock analysis, the longer the time frame, the stronger the credibility of the data and stock performance analysis. When analyzing stock performance, if the time frame is too short, other factors can have an impact on the stock price. The common denominator for the stocks in this book is their presence on the DiversityInc Top 50 List, which will be discussed in the next chapter.

Evolve and Succeed
- Recruitment and retention
  - Does your diversity recruiting program provide your company with qualified candidates thus reducing your expenses on recruiting and retention efforts?

DIVERSITY METRICS AND MEASUREMENT OF EVOLUTION

- Compliance
  - Does your diversity department implement polices and programs that reduce your exposure to litigation or affirmative action audits?
- Employment Engagement
  - Do your diversity department and policies increase job satisfaction, thus reducing the level of employee turnover?
  - Does the reduced employee turnover result in less open positions and lower recruiting expenses?
  - Do fewer open positions result in less training efforts for new employees that require up to one year of training to become fully functional at their job?

CHAPTER 9

THE CONNECTION TO DIVERSITY AND THE STOCK MARKET

"Natural selection follows from the struggle for existence; and this from a rapid rate of increase."

— Charles Darwin *The Descent of Man*

The stock market has its own economic ecosystem. Similar to plants and animals in nature struggling to survive, stocks are created (listed), thrive (increase in value), reproduce (split and add offerings), and die (delist, liquidate, or go bankrupt). The comparisons of Darwin's principles of natural selection and diversity also relate to the guiding principles of those that govern stock market movement.

Just as the natural environment cannot support all living things in the ecosystem without the presence of death to balance the strain on the system, the stock market cannot possibly support all of the stocks that have been created over time without the removal of weaker stocks. There must be winners and losers, outperformers and underperformers, and the ratings that estimate performance based on upgrades, downgrades, and neutrals. For the stock market to properly function, the removal of weaker, underperforming stocks is required.

To use the Darwin quote for this chapter, "natural selection follows from the struggle for existence; and this from a rapid rate of increase," the stock market cannot support a scenario where all stocks are winners and

THE CONNECTION TO DIVERSITY AND THE STOCK MARKET

outperformers. Each business with a publicly traded stock is in a struggle to outperform the market. This takes us back to one of the core facts of this book: 89% of the Fortune 500 companies in existence in 1955 were no longer in existence in 2013. Publicly traded companies are in a constant struggle for financing, investors, market share, customers, and the latest technology to ensure a rapid rate of increase in their stock price. The constant absence of these factors, or failure to manage them properly, often results in a decrease in business and stock price. The struggle for existence also includes the proper reaction to the general economic environment.

Artificial Interference with Evolution

The great recession created a harsh economic environment that caused many companies to face extinction. According to Forbes, the great recession led to the extinction of companies worth billions, including:

- Lehman Brothers   Assets: $691.1 billion
- Washington Mutual   Assets: $327.9 billion
- Colonial BancGroup   Assets: $25.8 billion
- Guaranty Financial Group   Assets: $16.8 billion

These four companies alone equal $1,061,600 trillion!

During the great recession, companies and journalists created and used the phrase "too big to fail." Too big to fail was really corporate speak for "we messed up and are facing extinction. Uncle Sam, please save us." Too big to fail goes against evolution and natural selection as many large companies should have evolved or faced extinction. After all, were massive dinosaurs to big to fail? In the spirit of Darwin, many of these companies would have faced extreme pain, evolved, and adapted. So fearing how the recession would hurt the US taxpayer, according to Propublica, the US government bailed out 956 companies for a total of $619 billion of US taxpayer dollars. The top ten recipients of bailout dollars include:

DIVERSIFY OR DIE: DIVERSITY. INCLUSION. EVOLUTION. SUCCESS.

Company Name	Amount Disbursed
Fannie Mae	$116,149,000,000
Freddie Mac	$71,336,000,000
AIG	$67,835,000,000
General Motors	$50,744,648,329
Bank of America	$45,000,000,000
Citigroup	$45,000,000,000
J.P. Morgan Chase	$25,000,000,000
Wells Fargo	$25,000,000,000
GMAC (now Ally Financial)	$16,290,000,000
Chrysler	$10,748,284,222

One could argue the US government bailouts interfered with natural selection, as the companies should have been allowed to face extinction. However, natural selection is not one-dimensional—when one species dies, many others may die as well.

Without government bailouts, a number of cities would have lost a lot more jobs and tax dollars. Loss of jobs and tax dollars also means loss of services, foreclosures, and people moving out of the area to seek work in other cities. When people move out of the area, businesses lose customers and may fail. Again, natural selection at work. The most common example is the bailout of the automotive industry and the direct impact the bailout had in protecting Detroit, MI, from financial ruin. Notice, General Motors and Chrysler are numbers four and ten on the Propublica list, respectively.

The Analysis of Diversity and the Stock Market

How can diversity be linked to stock performance? In theory, there are many ways to conduct this analysis. In the article, "Competitiveness Through Management of Diversity: Effects on Stock Evaluation," published in the Academy of Management Journal, the authors argue that quality affirmative action programs benefit the organization and have a positive financial impact that results in investors valuing the stock more highly. This article was published in 1995, when affirmative action was at the forefront of the diversity conversation. The article recognizes that affirmative action is "a dimension in the management of diversity."

THE CONNECTION TO DIVERSITY AND THE STOCK MARKET

The authors used companies that were awarded the US Department of Labor's Office of Federal Contract Compliance Programs (OFCCP) Exemplary Voluntary Efforts (EVE) Award as the sample for this analysis. In the author analysis, the companies had to be listed in the New York Stock Exchange or American Stock Exchange. The authors reasoned the positive announcement of the EVE Award and the public nature of the award had a positive impact on stock prices. It is important to note that the OFCCP issued Directive 312 on August 6, 2013, which ended the EVE award program. The last EVE awards were in 2008.

The research showed the Department of Labor's announcement of the EVE Award was associated with "significant and positive excess returns that represent the capitalization of positive information concerning improved business prospects." The research analyzes the stock performance of EVE awardees weeks before and after the award announcement. This was a very limited time frame. Also, as the EVE Award was not consistently awarded to the same company every year, the analysis of the stock price was based on the company's diversity efforts in the same year as the award receipt rather than diversity efforts that have evolved over a long period of time.

The *Diversify or Die* Stock Analysis, which covers 2001 – 2016, uses public information to compare the stock prices of companies recognized for their efforts in diversity to the overall stock market and their peers. Excerpts from each company's annual report or information from their websites were used verbatim.

The Diversify or Die Stock Analysis
This chapter sets forth the *Diversify or Die* Stock Analysis. The method used to conduct the D*iversify or Die* Stock Analysis follows.

There are thousands of publicly traded stocks. Since the number of publicly traded stocks is too large for an analysis, the first step in the Diversify or Die Stock Analysis is to find a common characteristic for comparison. The common characteristic narrows the number of stocks in the analysis to a more reasonable number. The common characteristic we chose is that all stocks were awarded a place on the "DiversityInc Top 50 Companies for Diversity."

DIVERSIFY OR DIE: DIVERSITY. INCLUSION. EVOLUTION. SUCCESS.

DiversityInc

Founded in 1998, DiversityInc is a content-based website and magazine that is published five times per year. DiversityInc's mission is to "bring education and clarity to the business benefits of diversity." Every year, DiversityInc publishes a report that names the top fifty companies for diversity. The companies on the "DiversityInc Top 50" include both public and private companies across many sectors, including: finance, healthcare, communications, insurance, consumer goods, manufacturing, and energy.

The DiversityInc Top 50 Companies for Diversity List began in 2001. This is the same time many corporations were beginning to understand the business value of managing diversity. Similar to the practice of diversity, the DiversityInc Top 50 List has evolved significantly and continues to reflect how rapidly companies are adapting these strategies.

Placing on the Diversity Top 50 is challenging. The selection process assesses overall performance of all applicants in four key areas of diversity management:

- Talent Pipeline: workforce breakdown, recruitment, diameter of existing talent, and structures
- Equitable Talent Development: employee resource groups, mentoring, philanthropy, movement, and fairness
- CEO/Leadership Commitment: accountability for results, personal communications, and visibility
- Supplier Diversity: spend with companies owned by people from underrepresented groups, accountability, and support

The DiversityInc Top 50 process is editorially driven and applicants do not pay for the application and selection. The DiversityInc Top 50 List is chosen from corporate survey submissions and analyzes publicly traded and privately held companies from 2001 – 2016. DiversityInc reports that the number of applications increases every year. In 2014, DiversityInc received 1,215 applications. That means in 2014, each company had a .04% chance in making the Top 50 List.

THE CONNECTION TO DIVERSITY AND THE STOCK MARKET

Finally, it is important to note all the information on the DiversityInc process and DiversityInc Top 50 List is based on public information. DiversityInc has not contributed to, or approved of this information in this book.

Public v. Privately Owned Companies

There are many excellent privately owned companies on the DiversityInc Top 50 List. As the focus of this chapter is a comparison between diversity programs in publicly traded companies, the analysis compares the selected company's stock performance to their stock market index and sector.

The DiversityInc Top 50 List publicly traded stocks are in one of three stock market indexes: New York Stock Exchange (NYSE), NASDAQ, and American Stock Exchange (AMEX). The *Diversify or Die* Stock Analysis follows the stock performance in their individual stock exchange as compared to the performance of the Standard and Poors 500 (S&P 500), the 500 companies in the USA with the largest market capitalization.

Technical Factors and Fundamental Factors

When looking at the past performance of stocks to predict the future performance, investors look at many factors, including technical factors and fundamental factors.

Technical factors focus on the price of the stock as it forms certain patterns in a stock chart. These patterns are used to speculate the future performance of the stock. Fundamental factors focus on the fundamentals of the business, including:

- CEO and senior leadership,
- Profit and loss statements,
- Quarterly reports,
- Sales reports,
- Research, and
- Development pipeline, expected innovations, etc.

DIVERSIFY OR DIE: DIVERSITY. INCLUSION. EVOLUTION. SUCCESS.

The *Diversify or Die* Stock Analysis is based on stock chart technical factors to analyze the past performance of DiversityInc Top 50 stocks for a number of reasons.

1. The *Diversify or Die* Stock Analysis is strictly for historical purposes, not to speculate on future performance. Stock graphs quickly convey the historical stock performance. Use of fundamentals in the stock analysis may call for interpretation and speculation on events in the business and how it impacted the stock price. The most consistent data, and the least common denominator, is to compare the performance of the individual stock to performance to the stock market index where the stock is located.
2. Stock prices rise and fall for many reasons on any given day. In the *Diversify or Die* Stock Analysis, the overall trend of a stock is the most important factor. The overall trend can show upward and downward spikes, highs and lows, which way the stock is trending, and the price of the stock at any given time in the charted time frame.
3. The stock chart visibly compares the stock to the applicable index. By charting a comparison on the same graph, the performance of the stock can show a direct comparison to the performance of the index. This is an excellent way to compare the long-term performance of the stock to the index.

Top 10 of the DiversityInc Top 50 from 2001 – 2016

Companies in the *Diversify or Die* Stock Analysis were ranked by the number of years they were on the DiversityInc Top 50 List. The more years the companies were on the list, the higher their ranking on the Diversify or Die Stock Analysis, regardless of their position on the Top 50 List for each year. Companies that have been on the Top 50 List thirteen through sixteen years immediately rose to the top of our list. When companies were on the list for the same number of years, they were also rated by their ranking for each year. The companies closer to the top of the list in the sixteen years were ranked higher in a tie.

THE CONNECTION TO DIVERSITY AND THE STOCK MARKET

The *Diversify or Die* Stock Analysis list is not a recommendation to purchase the stock or speculation the stock price will increase in value in any way. It is a historical analysis of the past performance of the stock as compared to the S&P 500 and stock index with diversity as the backdrop.

Reading the Diversify or Die Stock Charts

Google Finance is the source of the data for the *Diversify or Die* Stock Analysis and stock charts. The *Diversify or Die* Stock Charts are designed for the reader that does not have any experience in investing or trading stocks or indexes. As such, the stocks are designed to convey the basic and critical information to support the stock analysis. As the DiversityInc Top 50 List started in 2001, the Y-Axis also starts in 2001 and ends in 2016. The numbers along the X-Axis represent the growth of money invested in the various stocks or indexes assuming an initial investment of $10,000 in each stock.

Five of the stocks in the *Diversify or Die* Stock Analysis: Wells Fargo, Marriot International, Verizon Communications, Prudential Financial, and International Business Machines represent the only stocks in their industries. By comparison, Proctor and Gamble, Coca-Cola and Colgate Palmolive are all in the The Dow Jones US Consumer Goods Index while Abbott Laboratories and Merck and Co., Inc. are in the The Dow Jones US Health Care Index. All of the stocks that are in the same index are included in the same graph.

Disclaimer
The stock analysis in this chapter is only for the diversity analysis, and must not be used as the basis of any investment decision. Nothing in this chapter should be construed as investment or financial advice. All stock investors should make such investigations as they deem necessary to arrive at an independent evaluation of an investment in the securities of the companies referred to in this book (including the merits and risks involved), and should consult their own advisors to determine the merits and risks of such an investment.

The views contained in this book are those of the author. Reports based on technical and derivative analysis center on studying charts of a stock's price movement, outstanding positions, and trading volume, as opposed to focusing on a company's fundamentals and, as such, may not match with a report on a company's fundamentals. The information in this document has been printed on the basis of publicly available information, annual reports, and other reliable sources believed to be true, but we do not represent that it is accurate or complete and it should not be relied on as such, as this document is for general guidance only.

The author, or any of the author's affiliates, shall not be in any way responsible for any loss or damage that may arise to any person from any inadvertent error in the information contained in this report. The author has not independently verified all the information contained within this document. Accordingly, the author cannot testify, nor make any representation or warranty, express or implied, to the accuracy, contents, or data contained within this document. Neither the author, nor the author's affiliates, shall be liable for any loss or damage that may arise from or in connection with the use of this information.

1. Wells Fargo & Company

Stock Symbol: WFC

Stock Exchange: NYSE

Index: S&P 500

Number of Years on the DiversityInc Top 50 List: 16

Wells Fargo & Company is a nationwide, diversified, community-based financial services company with $1.7 trillion in assets. Wells Fargo provides banking, insurance, investments, mortgage, and consumer and commercial finance through more than 8,700 locations, 12,500 ATMs, the Internet, and mobile banking. Wells Fargo has offices in 36 countries and approximately 265,000 active, full-time equivalent team members.

Diversity Statement/Mission
   Making diversity and inclusion part of our DNA
   As a nation, we are becoming more diverse, so much so that the U.S.

THE CONNECTION TO DIVERSITY AND THE STOCK MARKET

Census Bureau projects that by 2043 we will be a nation without an ethnic or racial majority. This is why it is critical that our team members reflect the diversity in our communities, so we can better understand and serve the needs of our customers. Internally, we nurture our diverse and inclusive culture in many ways. I personally chair our Diversity and Inclusion Council and have seen firsthand the advantages of having a culture that respects and values team members for who they are and the creativity and innovation that come from multiple perspectives and experiences. Our multicultural focus starts at the top. It is no coincidence that we have one of the most diverse boards of directors in the industry: Of our 15 directors, 10 are women and/or people of color. I also hold each of my direct reports accountable through a "diversity scorecard" that I review with them to track our progress. We offer comprehensive diversity and inclusion education for team members and sponsor 10 Team Member Networks that provide professional and leadership development, mentoring, and community involvement opportunities

Wells Fargo made the Top 50 List every year since the List's inception. On December 31, 2008, Wells Fargo closed on the purchase of Wachovia Corporation. Wachovia Corporation appeared on the DiversityInc Top 50 List four times: 2003, 2005, 2006, and 2007.

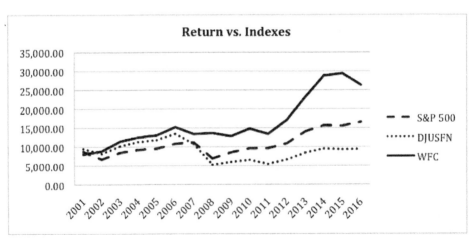

Wells Fargo consistently outperformed the S&P500 from 2003 to 2016 and further widened the gap in 2013. Wells Fargo stock closely mirrored but outperformed the Dow Jones Financials Index (DJUSFN), until 2006 when the DJUSFN declined compared to Wells Fargo.

DIVERSIFY OR DIE: DIVERSITY. INCLUSION. EVOLUTION. SUCCESS.

2. Marriott International

Stock Symbol: MAR

Stock Exchange: NASDAQ

Index: S&P 500

Number of Years on the DiversityInc Top 50 List: 15

Marriott International (Marriott), a lodging brand and travel company, has over 4,100 properties in 79 countries. Marriott has $14 billion in revenue and 360,000 employees in owner operated and franchised properties.

Diversity Statement/Mission

About Marriott—Diversity and Inclusion (Marriott.com):
Since 1927, Marriott has valued diversity and inclusion. Embracing differences is part of the way we do business around the world, and essential to our success as a leading hospitality company with a growing global portfolio. Diversity and inclusion are closely tied to our core values and our strategic business goals, so they are embedded into every facet of our business.

At Marriott, we know that it is essential for our leaders to truly embrace and understand different cultures. Nearly 70 percent of our hotel rooms under construction are beyond North America's shores. As we evolve our diversity and inclusion goals to support global growth, Marriott's core value of "putting people first" creates new opportunities in communities around the world.

Marriott's *"2014 Report on Global Diversity and Inclusion"* states:
Marriott International's Global Diversity and Inclusion (D&I) approach is deeply rooted in our company's culture and core values. Our culture is best represented by the first and most significant of our five core values, Put People First, including an emphasis on providing opportunity. Valuing and embracing differences is also a part of the way we do business every day around the world, and essential to

THE CONNECTION TO DIVERSITY AND THE STOCK MARKET

our success as a leading hospitality company with a growing global portfolio of more than 4,000 hotels in nearly 80 countries. We realized long ago that a diverse and inclusive workforce strengthens Marriott's culture and provides a competitive advantage. Our commitment to diversity and inclusion also enhances sustainable business growth, as well as economic and social vitality.

Marriott International made the Top 50 List fifteen out of sixteen years. The only year Marriott International did not make the list was 2002.

Marriott Stock Chart Analysis

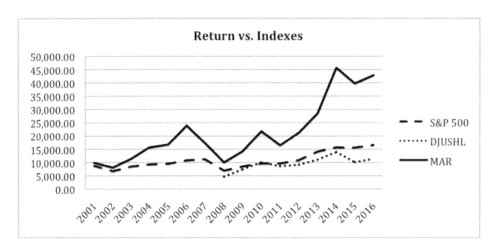

Overall, Marriott outperformed the S&P 500. In late 2008 and early 2009, Marriott's stock price declined but since then vastly outperformed the S&P 500. Marriott's stock has consistently outperformed the Dow Jones US Hotel & Lodging REITs Index (DJUSHL), which started in 2008.

3. Verizon Communications

Stock Symbol: VZ

Stock Exchange: NYSE

Index: S&P 500

Number of Years on the DiversityInc Top 50 List: 15

Verizon Communications, Inc. (Verizon) provides communications, information and entertainment products and services to consumers, businesses, and governmental agencies. Verizon offers voice, data, and video services and solutions on wireless and wireline networks.

Verizon has two reportable segments, Wireless and Wireline. The wireless business, operating as Verizon Wireless, provides voice and data services and equipment sales across the United States. Verizon's Wireline business provides consumer, business, and government customers with communications products and enhanced services, including broadband data and video, corporate networking solutions, data center and cloud services, security and managed network services, and local and long distance voice services.

Diversity Statement/Mission

Who We Are—Diversity and Inclusion (Verizon.com):

Verizon is committed to fostering an inclusive environment. We care about diversity in both our employees and our suppliers. Diversity and inclusion is how we achieve success. By celebrating diversity across all spectrums, including but not limited to race, national origin, religion, gender, sexual orientation, gender identity, disability, veteran/ military status, and age, we are a stronger company and culture.

We take pride in our talented and diverse team of people who focus on our customers, every day. Their combined intelligence, spirit, and creativity make Verizon a great place to work, learn, and grow.

THE CONNECTION TO DIVERSITY AND THE STOCK MARKET

Verizon made the Top 50 List every year except 2016 and was the number one company on the Top 50 List in 2006 and 2009.

Verizon Stock Chart Analysis

According to the stock analysis, Verizon Wireless has consistently outperformed the Dow Jones US Telecommunication Index (DJUSTL) market since 2003 and the S&P 500 since 2007.

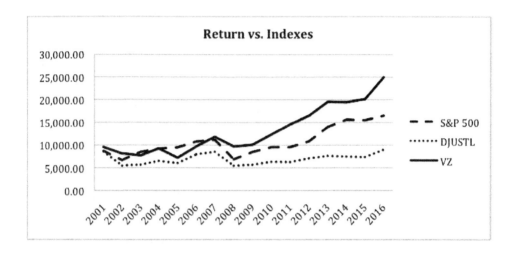

4. Prudential Financial

Stock Symbol: PRU

Stock Exchange: NYSE

Index: S&P 500

Number of Years on the DiversityInc Top 50 List: 15

Prudential Financial, Inc. (Prudential) offers individual and institutional clients a wide array of financial products and services. Prudential's 2014 Annual Report *"PRU 2014 Who We Are,"* states that Prudential has more than $1 trillion in assets under management and approximately $3.5 trillion of gross life insurance as of December 31, 2014. Prudential has operations in the United States, Asia, Europe, and Latin America.

Diversity Statement/Mission

"Our Commitment to Diversity" (Corporate.Prudential.com):
Difference can make all the difference in the world. At Prudential we count on that. We have a long-standing commitment to diversity in our workplace and marketplace.

We understand that we succeed through people—those who skillfully create and deliver the products and services that distinguish us from our competitors, those who confidently entrust their family's wealth protection and growth to us, those who invest in our company's future to help secure their own, and those who live alongside us on the city streets and neighborhood blocks where we do business.

With businesses in more than 40 countries, our company seeks talented, creative individuals from a variety of backgrounds, worldviews, and life circumstances to work with us. It is our priority that our workplace be inclusive, welcoming of new ideas, and appreciative of valuable experience.

Our business strategies fully consider, respect, and reach out to diverse

THE CONNECTION TO DIVERSITY AND THE STOCK MARKET

consumers and communities. Our goal is to partner with them to meet their current needs, support their dreams, and build their futures.

As the Leadership Team, we recognize that individual differences represent a mosaic of opportunities for Prudential. We hold ourselves, our management team, and all employees accountable for promoting an environment that values these differences and capitalizes on these opportunities for the ultimate benefit of our customers, shareholders, and employees.

Prudential, made the Top 50 List every year except 2016.

Prudential Stock Chart Analysis

Prudential consistently outperformed the S&P 500 from 2002 – 2016. Prudential's stock price dramatically decreased from 2007 to 2008 due to the financial crisis, but did not decrease as much as the Dow Jones Select Insurance Index (DJSINS) or the S&P 500. By 2009, Prudential rebounded to greatly outperform the S&P 500 and the DJSINS.

The chart above clearly demonstrates that the Financial Crisis of 2008 created a difficult operating environment for banking and insurance companies. This difficulty lasted for eighteen months. Nevertheless, Prudential maintained positive relative strength compared to its peers in the Dow Jones US Select Insurance Index (DJSINS) throughout the entire period.

5. Proctor & Gamble

Stock Symbol: PG

Stock Exchange: NYSE

Index: S&P 500

Number of Years on the DiversityInc Top 50 List: 13

Proctor & Gamble (P&G) is a global leader in fast-moving consumer goods that is focused on providing branded consumer packaged goods. P&G products are sold in more than 180 countries and territories primarily through mass merchandisers, grocery stores, membership club stores, drug stores, distributors, e-commerce, high-frequency stores, and pharmacies. P&G has operations in approximately 70 countries.

Diversity Statement/Mission
***"Diversity and Inclusion"* (US.PG.com):**
Fulfilling our Potential
Diversity and Inclusion is deeply rooted in our Purpose, Values, and Principles. It is who we are and who we aspire to be.

Every P&G employee is equally talented in unique ways. Beyond the visible differences, we come from diverse traditions, personal experiences, and points of view. That's why, in our increasingly interconnected world, it is only appropriate that we celebrate everyone's uniqueness, every day.

Our mission of Diversity and Inclusion is: "Everyone valued. Everyone included. Everyone performing at their peakTM."

P&G made the list thirteen out of sixteen years. The only years P&G did not make the list were 2001, 2003, and 2006.

THE CONNECTION TO DIVERSITY AND THE STOCK MARKET

Proctor & Gamble Stock Chart Analysis

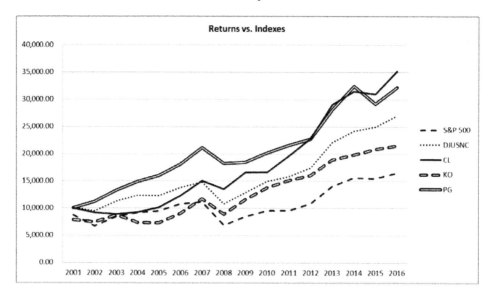

P&G outperformed the S&P 500 and The Dow Jones US Consumer Goods Index (DJUSNC) from 2001 to 2016. This index includes two others in our list: Coca-Cola (KO) and Colgate Palmolive (CL).

6. International Business Machines

Stock Symbol: IBM

Stock Exchange: NYSE

Index: S&P 500

Number of Years on the DiversityInc Top 50 List: 13

International Business Machines (IBM) provides integrated solutions and products that leverage data, information technology, deep expertise in industries and business processes, and a broad ecosystem of partners and alliances. These solutions draw from an industry-leading portfolio of consulting and IT implementation services, cloud and cognitive offerings, and enterprise systems and software; all bolstered by one of the world's leading research organizations. (2014 Annual Report)

Diversity Statement/Mission
"Diversity and Inclusion" **(IBM.com):**

> *IBM's enduring commitment to diversity is one of the reasons we can credibly say that IBM is one of the world's leading globally integrated enterprises. We also understand that diversity goes beyond fair hiring practices and protection for all employees. It also includes a focus on how those disparate pieces fit together to create an innovative, integrated whole. We call this approach "inclusion."*

> *While our differences shape who we are as individual IBMers, our shared corporate culture and values remain central to our mutual success. IBMers around the world work in an environment where diversity—including diversity of thought—is the norm, which yields a commitment to creating client innovation in every part of our business.*

IBM made the Top 50 List thirteen out of fourteen years. The only years IBM did not make the list were 2005, 2006, and 2007.

THE CONNECTION TO DIVERSITY AND THE STOCK MARKET

IBM Stock Chart Analysis

IBM and the S&P 500 crossed paths in 2005, but from 2005 to 2016, IBM outperformed the S&P 500. IBM consistently outperformed the Dow Jones US Technology Index (DJUSTC) from 2001 – 2016.

DIVERSIFY OR DIE: DIVERSITY. INCLUSION. EVOLUTION. SUCCESS.

7. Abbott Laboratories

Stock Symbol: ABT

Stock Exchange: NYSE

Index: S&P 500

Number of Years on the DiversityInc Top 50 List: 13

Abbott Laboratories is a globally diversified healthcare company whose central purpose is to help people at all stages of life that align with favorable long-term healthcare trends in both developed and developing markets. *(2014 Annual Report)*

Diversity Statement/Mission

"An Inclusive Culture" **contains a quote from Miles D. White, Chairman & CEO, Abbott (Abbott.com):**

> *The business case for a diverse workplace is clear: companies with more diversity among their people think more creatively and adapt more quickly to changing markets. We're a global company; we need a wide diversity of ideas and perspectives to understand the people we serve and be relevant to their lives.*

Abbott Laboratories, a major health care seller and manufacturer, made the Top 50 List thirteen out of sixteen years. The only years Abbott Laboratories did not make the list were 2001, 2002, and 2003.

THE CONNECTION TO DIVERSITY AND THE STOCK MARKET

Abbott Laboratories Stock Chart Analysis

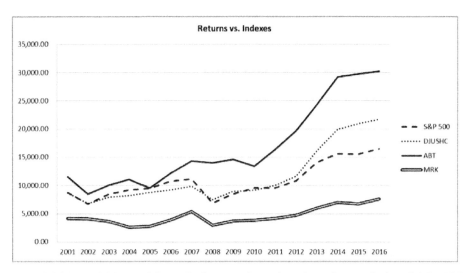

From 2001 to 2005, Abbott Laboratories closely mirrored the S&P 500. Abbott Laboratories and the S&P crossed paths in 2005, then from 2005 to 2016 Abbott Laboratories outperformed the S&P 500. From 2001 to 2016 Abbott Laboratories consistently outperformed the Dow Jones US Health Care Index (DJUSHC), Also, Abbott Laboratories did not experience the same decrease as the S&P 500 and the DJUSHC during the 2008 – 2009 recession.

8. Merck & Co., Inc.

Stock Symbol: MRK

Stock Exchange: NYSE

Index: S&P 500

Number of Years on the DiversityInc Top 50 List: 13

Merck & Co., Inc. (Merck) is a global health care company that delivers innovative health solutions. Merck has four operating segments: Pharmaceutical, Animal Health, Alliances, and Healthcare Services. *(2015 Annual Report)*

Diversity Statement/Mission

"Employee Diversity" (Merck.com):
> *Diversity and inclusion are integrated into our leadership model, and are considered an essential leadership skill for all of our employees. We expect all employees, beginning with our leaders, to achieve diversity and inclusion goals, which are used to gauge individual and company performance. We define, measure, and reward diversity performance through a number of tools, including affirmative action plans and diversity objectives on our company scorecard.*

Merck made the Top 50 List thirteen out of sixteen years. The only years Merck did not make the list were 2001, 2002, and 2008.

THE CONNECTION TO DIVERSITY AND THE STOCK MARKET

Merck & Co., Inc. Stock Chart Analysis

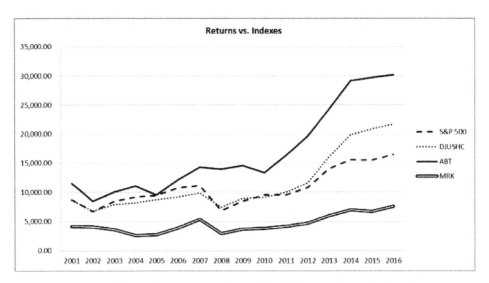

Merck underperformed compared to the S&P 500 and the Dow Jones US Health Care Index (DJUSHC), which includes Abbott Laboratories (evaluated earlier).

DIVERSIFY OR DIE: DIVERSITY. INCLUSION. EVOLUTION. SUCCESS.

9. Coca-Cola Company

Stock Symbol: KO

Stock Exchange: NYSE

Index: S&P 500

Number of Years on the DiversityInc Top 50 List: 13

The Coca-Cola Company (Coca-Cola) is the world's largest beverage company with more than 500 sparkling and still brands. Coca-Cola has consumers in more than 200 countries that drink beverages at a rate of 1.9 billion servings a day. Including bottling partners, Coca-Cola employs more than 700,000 system associates.

Diversity Statement/Mission
"Global Diversity Mission" **(Coca-ColaCompany.com):**
The Coca-Cola Company's global diversity mission is to mirror the rich diversity of the marketplace we serve and be recognized for our leadership in Diversity, Inclusion, and Fairness in all aspects of our business, including Workplace, Marketplace, Supplier, and Community, enhancing the Company's social license to operate.

Diversity is at the heart of our business. We strive to create a work environment that provides all our associates equal access to information, development, and opportunity. By building an inclusive workplace environment, we seek to leverage our global team of associates, which is rich in diverse people, talent, and ideas. We see diversity as more than just policies and practices. It is an integral part of who we are as a company, how we operate, and how we see our future.

THE CONNECTION TO DIVERSITY AND THE STOCK MARKET

Coca-Cola Stock Chart Analysis

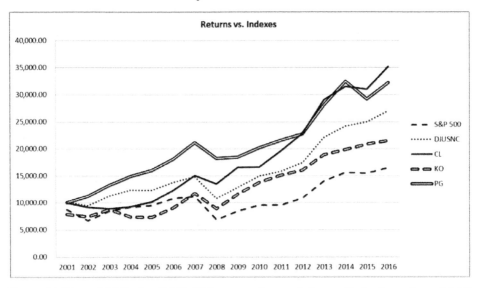

From 2003 to 2007, the S&P 500 outperformed Coca-Cola; but since 2007, Coca-Cola has out performed the S&P 500.

Like Proctor & Gamble (PG) and Colgate Palmolive (CL: discussed next), Coca-Cola is a component of the Dow Jones US Consumer Goods Index (DJUSCG). The DJUSCG outperformed Coca-Cola from 2001.

10. Colgate Palmolive

Stock Symbol: CL

Stock Exchange: NYSE

Index: S&P 500

Number of Years on the DiversityInc Top 50 List: 13

Colgate Palmolive, a consumer products company, markets products in over 200 countries and territories throughout the world. Colgate, best known for their oral care products, also has personal and home care products as well as pet nutrition.

Diversity Statement/Mission
"Our Company: Living Our Values" (Colgate.com):
Unique Differences
Colgate's success is created by Colgate people who work together as a worldwide team, using their individual strengths to achieve business results. This strong global teamwork requires a company culture in which everyone works well together and truly values one another. We support an environment where everyone's ideas are shared and respected. At Colgate, we want people to feel energized and encouraged to contribute to their fullest potential.

The diversity of Colgate people around the world is vital to finding new solutions to business challenges and new opportunities from unique insights. Differences are recognized and appreciated as the traits that make each of us who we are. We celebrate diversity in our people because we know that it is these differences that are foundations of our continued achievement

THE CONNECTION TO DIVERSITY AND THE STOCK MARKET

Colgate Palmolive made the Top 50 List thirteen out of sixteen years. The only years Colgate Palmolive did not make the list were 2002, 2003, and 2008.

Colgate Palmolive Stock Chart Analysis

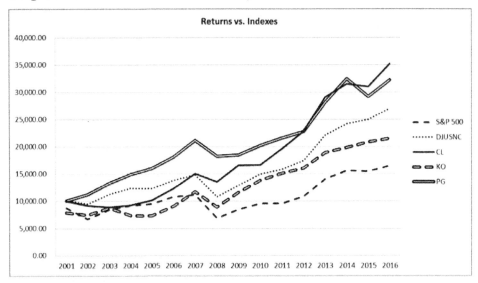

Colgate Palmolive mirrored the S&P 500 from 2003 to 2005 and then consistently outperformed the S&P 500. The DJUSNC outperformed Colgate form 2001 to 2007, after which Colgate outperformed the DJUSNC.

Colgate Palmolive is another member of the Consumer Goods Sector, which for the period studied was the third best group analyzed. And, as the chart below explains, Colgate Palmolive is the last of the companies on the DiversityInc Top 50 List studied in the *Diversify or Die* Stock Analysis outperformed compared to its peer group, which includes Coca-Cola (KO) and Colgate Palmolive (CL).

DIVERSIFY OR DIE: DIVERSITY. INCLUSION. EVOLUTION. SUCCESS.

Overall Diversified Portfolio Returns

The S&P 500 and each of the seven sector indices used in the *Diversify or Die* Stock Analysis represent, for the most part, diversified baskets of stocks. In essence, each of these indices is a diversified stock portfolio. As such, it is reasonable to consider the ten stocks studied in the *Diversify or Die* Stock Analysis as a diversified stock portfolio. Thus, we back-tested a portfolio made up of the ten stocks studied above.

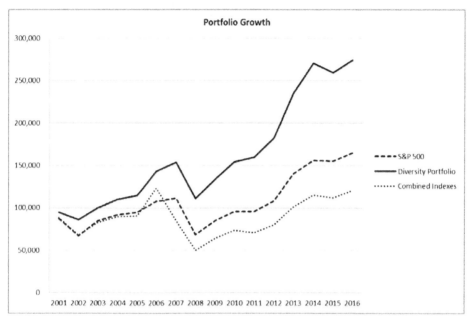

The Diversify or Die Stock Analysis assumed an initial investment of $100,000 equally divided between each of the stocks (e.g., $10,000 per company). We compared that to an equal $100,000 investment in the S&P 500. We used the State Street Advisors SPDR S&P 500 ETF (NYSE: SPY) to represent the market. With that as our premise, how then did this "Diversify or Die Portfolio" hold up to the overall market from 2001 to 2016?

The answer is actually—very well! From January 2001 through July 2016, the Compound Annual Growth Rate (CAGR) of our Diversify or Die Portfolio beat the total return of the S&P 500 by 3.1% (7.54% to 4.47%). As a result, the Diversify or Die Portfolio would have earned an investor an additional $100,541 than an investment in the S&P 500.

THE CONNECTION TO DIVERSITY AND THE STOCK MARKET

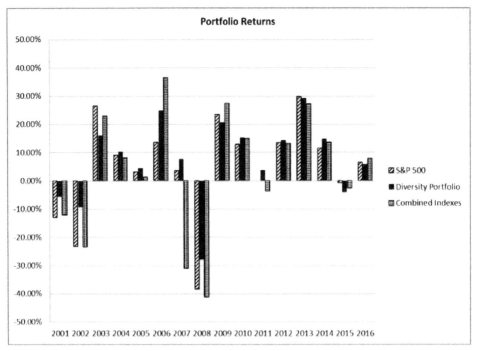

More importantly, as shown in the above graph, the *Diversify or Die* Portfolio would have subjected a long-term buy-and-hold investor with lower volatility and a lower loss in carrying value during the eighteen months of the financial crisis. The solid black bar graphs show that during recession years, 2001, 2002 and 2008, that the Diversify or Die Portfolio did not decrease as much as the S&P 500 or the Combined Indexes.

Overall Stock Analysis Summary
There are many ways to interpret a stock chart. The Diversify or Die Stock Analysis does not create a utopian analysis of the ten stocks to unrealistically argue that diversity is the perfect solution to create profit for any business. A few of the stocks in the *Diversify or Die* Stock Analysis underperformed the S&P 500 at some point in time since 2001. All of the Diversify or Die Stock Analysis companies survived the great recession, and recovered, some reaching new highs in their stock price. But diversity is a marathon, not a sprint, and that also applies to the *Diversify or Die* Stock Analysis.

DIVERSIFY OR DIE: DIVERSITY. INCLUSION. EVOLUTION. SUCCESS.

Underutilization of Diversity and Underperforming Stocks

What if your company stock is underperforming compared to the S&P 500 or the index where your stock resides? What if your stock is underperforming compared to the industrial index where your stock resides? One of the reasons your stock is underperforming may be because your company does not have active, progressive, and ongoing diversity efforts. This is a good time to review the same questions we addressed in Chapter 6 about the quality of your diversity program.

- Where is the department housed? Is it in HR?
- How is it staffed? Experienced diversity professionals?
- Is the diversity department adequately staffed and funded?
- Does the diversity department work with other departments on critical organizational objectives?
- Does the diversity department have access to the CEO?

If your diversity efforts are lacking in one or more of these areas, this could be one of the reasons your company is underperforming in your company's index.

The improvement in diversity and inclusion efforts is not the only way to improve stock performance, but it is one way that the board of directors should seriously consider. If a long-term strategy is not on the agenda, then the board of directors is not considering all of its viable options.

Once again, this takes us back to the diversity equation and definition of diversity.

The business practice to increase the bottom line by capitalizing on the responsible sale and distribution of goods or services to multicultural clientele and the supportive employment of multicultural employees at all levels of the organization.

As this generic definition is designed for all types of organizations, it is more applicable if the definition is designed for a publicly traded company.

THE CONNECTION TO DIVERSITY AND THE STOCK MARKET

The business practice to increase profit and market share by responsibly selling consumer goods and services to a diverse clientele and the supportive employment of multicultural employees at all levels of the company.

The inclusion of profit and market share in the definition of diversity directly links the importance of diversity to the success of the publicly traded company. The definition also shows the impact of increased sales and market share to stock price. Of course the impact on the stock price will not be immediate and may take years after a fully functional diversity program is in effect, but it is a step in the direction of evolution for the company.

Evolve and Succeed

- If your company stock is underperforming in your stock index, consider increasing your resources and funding into long-term diversity and inclusion efforts and directly combining diversity efforts to sales and marketing.
- Review your profit and loss statement and consider where long-term diversity efforts can increase company profits and decrease company losses.
- If your board of directors does not reflect your employee, client, and local or regional population, you are missing important voices on the board that will help you with diversity, inclusion, evolution, and success.
- Similar to your mission statement and core values, make sure your board knows the definition of diversity for your company or the diversity mission statement as all board decisions should have those diversity statements in mind.

CHAPTER 10
WORDS OF MOTIVATION FOR EVOLUTION

"Selfish and contentious people will not cohere, and without coherence nothing can be effected."

— Charles Darwin, *The Descent of Man*

So far this book has set forth a diversity equation, consistent diversity definitions, census numbers, income data, a diversity timeline, and a stock market analysis for ten stocks recognized for their diversity efforts. All of the diversity and inclusion components to improve an organization's bottom line have been presented except one: motivation. Specifically, motivating leaders, managers, and employees who do not want to use diversity and inclusion.

Motivating employees may be the most difficult component of improving diversity and inclusion in an organization. As discussed earlier, two factors that keep diversity from making evolutionary organizational change include the desire to keep power in its current form, and the practice of making decisions based on emotions rather than facts.

Words to Motivate Management Actions

Changing an employee's perspective on diversity and inclusion requires more than a few motivational words and usually more than one conversation. Based on my experience, it will probably take many conversations over a period of time.

WORDS OF MOTIVATION FOR EVOLUTION

When faced with a challenge to motivate managers to practice diversity, my first objective is to determine the reasons the manager does not practice diversity. The next step is to determine the best way to motivate the manager. The required motivation may be to change the heart and mind of the manager. One of the best ways to accomplish this is to show the manager that practicing diversity is one of the best ways to benefit the organization. Once motivated, one of the most difficult steps is for the manager to actually use diversity in their everyday management.

Use of diversity in everyday management is important, as employees pay more attention to what managers do than what they say. When managers lead by setting the example of diversity and inclusion, employees are more likely to follow. In addition to actions, motivational conversations and phrases can help employees evolve on their personal diversity journey.

Progressive Motivational Quotes

Using motivational quotes is a wonderful way to encourage self-improvement. You can find these quotes on many topics. I have personally found motivational quotes to be inspiring in a variety of areas. This chapter introduces the "progressive motivational quotes." Progressive motivational quotes starts by recognizing there may be a problem, then moves to understanding the problem, and then to resolving the problem.

Progressive motivational quotes presents one possible way to motivate managers and employees, but there are plenty other motivational quotes you can use to inspire your employees based on the needs of your organization. If the best way to start making progress in diversity programs is to motivate managers and employees, use the quotes that will best serve the problem at hand.

It isn't that they can't see the solution, it's that they can't see the problem.
—G.K. Chesterton, English writer, poet, and philosopher

There are many reasons problems cannot be "seen." One possible reason is unconscious bias. Bias is a behavior that will always be present. We all make split-second decisions that impact our daily lives and the lives around us.

DIVERSIFY OR DIE: DIVERSITY. INCLUSION. EVOLUTION. SUCCESS.

Our decisions are based on judgments (even small ones), past experiences, emotions, and many other factors. Many of these decisions are based in our unconscious mind. That is where unconscious bias comes in. So if we all have unconscious bias, how does that impact diversity?

Although we all use unconscious bias to make decisions, that decision impacts someone else if the decision maker has power over other people. This takes us back to the discussion about diversity and power in Chapter 1. From hiring managers that only hire applicants that look like them, to the realtor that only shows houses in certain areas to certain cultures and ethnicities, and the church pastor who preaches about love but excludes different sexual orientations from his/her congregation, there are many examples of the use of unconscious bias with power to impact the lives of others. Once unconscious bias and power are in play, diversity becomes part of the conversation.

As noted in the CDO Insights article, "Proven Strategies for Addressing Unconscious Bias in the Workplace," unconscious bias adds a new dimension to diversity. Before the recognition of unconscious bias, the practice of diversity and inclusion was based on correcting decisions made by the conscious mind. Diversity training and policies were focused on changing the behavior and decision making of employees and managers who were not able to embrace diversity. Unconscious bias recognizes those behaviors and that decision-making may be unconscious. This recognition is critical because it creates a safer space to discuss diversity and bring about organizational change. In supporting the presence of unconscious bias in organizations, "Proven Strategies for Addressing Unconscious Bias in the Workplace" states:

> *Organizational culture is more or less an enduring collection of basic assumptions and ways of interpreting things that a given organization has invented, discovered, or developed in learning to cope with its internal and external influences. Unconscious organization patterns, or "norms" of behavior, exert an enormous influence over organizational decisions, choices, and behaviors. These deep-seated company characteristics often are the reason that our efforts to change organizational behavior fail. Despite our best conscious efforts, the "organizational unconscious" perpetuates the status quo and keeps old patterns, values, and behavioral norms firmly rooted.*

Organizations are learning and evolving to address unconscious bias. From a generational perspective, it is important to note that "unconscious bias" has also been called "second generation discrimination." According to The Growing Business of Detecting Unconscious Bias," (2015) published in the *Wall Street Journal,* "as many as 20% of large US companies are providing unconscious bias training to their employees, and this percentage can reach 50% in the next five years."

Unconscious bias training for 50% of US companies would be an impressive accomplishment, but it would only be effective if the unconscious bias training were designed with the long-term objectives and goals of the organization in mind. In an article in the Harvard Business Review, "What Facebook's Anti-Bias Training Get's Right," author Francesca Gino raises an important point. Simply letting employees know they have unconscious bias is not enough. The training has to:

- Raise awareness and acceptance of the influence of bias,
- Stress concern about the consequence of bias, and
- Discuss strategies that eliminate unconscious bias and how to apply them

These training objectives are three very important learning points for each unconscious bias learner and will get things started. Once the conversation starts, unconscious bias begins to change to conscious bias and a conscious problem. Conscious problems can be solved.

Every problem is a gift—without problems we would not grow.
      —Anthony Robbins, Motivational Speaker and Writer

When organizations are honest and realize diversity may be a problem, the "gift of growth" has presented itself. But nothing worthwhile is easy. Whenever I train on diversity, I always tell the participants that there is no growth without discomfort. If we are in a constant state of comfort, there is no challenge. If there is no challenge, there is no struggle. If there is no struggle, there is no growth.

Muhammad Ali said, "I hated every minute of training, but I said 'Don't quit. Suffer now and live the rest of your life as a champion.'" That is one

DIVERSIFY OR DIE: DIVERSITY. INCLUSION. EVOLUTION. SUCCESS.

of the many reasons that Muhammad Ali was known as "The Greatest." Ali knew training was the key to defeating his opponents and staying The Greatest. The other reason was because Ali brought a new level of thinking and strategy to boxing. Ali's pre-bout strategies and tactics in the ring, my favorite being the rope-a-dope, evolved boxing to new levels. Ali turned the challenge of training into heavyweight championships and growth in boxing.

Of course, training for employees is not a heavyweight title match, but the failure to train employees can limit growth. To complicate this discussion, during my trainings I always tell participants that the failure to train employees to solve new and different problems ends up causing more problems! All managers want a highly educated, highly trained workforce, but many managers don't want to spend the money or give the employee the time to take required trainings. There are other organizations that will gladly train good employees, so the failure to train employees can lead to an unnecessary loss of a resource.

"Problems" come in many forms. In my experience, one of the most common forms is that related to discrimination, harassment, and retaliation investigations and lawsuits. It may seem difficult to view the problems of internal investigations, EEOC complaints, and lawsuits as gifts, but many organizations faced with very public legal diversity and discrimination issues used courageous leadership, progressive programs, and innovative training to emerge as stronger organizations. Denny's Restaurant, a subsidiary of FlagStar Companies that I mentioned in Chapter 3, is an excellent example of turning a diversity and discrimination problem into a gift of growth.

In 1994, Denny's Restaurants agreed to pay $54 million to settle lawsuits filed by black customers. The black customers alleged they had to wait longer for service, were refused service, were forced to prepay for their meals, and were treated rudely by Denny's employees. In one example, black Secret Service agents from President Clinton's detail were denied service while white Secret Service were seated and served. Denny's became known as a "racist restaurant." Anyone who does not believe that an employee, or group of employees, can expose the organization to extreme losses should keep in mind that waitresses, waiters, and restaurant owners cost Denny's

$54 million in settlements and more in lost business. But Denny's evolved and grew as a company by making big changes in hiring, supplier diversity, and training.

In 2002, a *FreeRepublic.com* article "Worst to First: Restaurant Chain Buries its Racist Image," reported an update on Denny's diversity and inclusion efforts after the settlement:
- Half of the parent company employees, forty-six thousand, were minorities (11% black and 31% Hispanic)
- Minorities held 32% of the supervisory positions
- Contracts with minority suppliers increased from zero in 1992 to $100 million per year in 2002
- The number of black franchises increased from one in 1992 to sixty-four in 2002
- Minority traffic increased to 61 million visitors in 2000 from 51 million in 1998, and system wide, including franchise revenues, sales in 2001 reached a record $2.23 billion.

Facing the possibility of extinction, Denny's evolved. A Lubbock Avalanche-Journal article quoted Ray Hood-Phillips, chief diversity officer for Denny's parent company, Advantica Restaurant as saying: "You will hear us all say here that that lawsuit was one of the best things that happened to Denny's." A powerful way to state, "Every problem is a gift—without problems we would not grow."

Strength and growth come only through continuous effort and struggle.
—Napoleon Hill, Author

Selfish and contentious employees do not put in the effort or struggle to grow the organization, they only think about themselves and their own agendas. While there may be times when the interests of the selfish and contentious employee may be the same as the organization, as soon as those common interests separate, the organization's interests fall to a distant second.

In previous chapters, we discussed the challenge where organizations give up on diversity and inclusion efforts because they do not work. As with any

DIVERSIFY OR DIE: DIVERSITY. INCLUSION. EVOLUTION. SUCCESS.

efforts to maintain a functional organization, leadership must be persistent to have diversity and inclusion efforts benefit the organization. Short term, underfunded, and understaffed diversity and inclusion efforts are doomed to fail from the start. Once diversity and inclusion efforts are given the proper resources, the next step is continuous effort and struggle.

In *Think & Grow Rich*, Napoleon Hill addresses continuous effort and struggle:

> *If the first plan which you adopt does not work successfully, replace it with a new plan, if this new plan fails to work, replace it, in turn with still another, and so on, until you find a plan which DOES WORK. Right here is the point at which the majority of [people] meet with failure, because of their lack of PERSISTENCE in creating new plans to take the place of those which fail. (Emphasis not added.)*

Growth is not immediate. The gift of growth is not a one-time fix or a short-term effort. It is a long-term, ongoing process. Growth in diversity requires the same long-term, ongoing commitment. The right path is for organizations to sufficiently fund and staff programs and not stop until one of the diversity programs actually works. The Denny's diversity story is a good example of a diversity plan that worked over the years.

The more we run from conflict, the more it masters us; the more we try to avoid it, the more it controls us; the less we fear conflict, the less it confuses us; the less we deny our differences, the less they divide us.
—David Augsburger, PhD, Author

This is an important quote for diversity and inclusion, as many organizations avoid diversity inclusion efforts expecting conflicts or disagreements when they may not even exist. The best approach is to embrace differences to create better teams, not to run from differences or allow them to divide a team.

Running from or avoiding conflict can take many forms, including finding excuses not to address diversity problems in the organization. As mentioned earlier in the book, the common running and avoiding excuses I have personally heard include:

WORDS OF MOTIVATION FOR EVOLUTION

- It is not a good time
- We don't have the money to invest in diversity programs
- We are downsizing, it would not look good to spend money on diversity
- We don't want to distract the employees with diversity efforts

Sound familiar? While these phrases are not using the words "running" and "avoiding," the results are the same. These phrases are simply politically correct excuses to keep the status quo. By now, you should realize that maintaining and accepting the "status quo" is the first step to extinction.

Hopefully at this time in the motivational journey, managers and employees are motivated to address diversity issues. If additional motivation is required, the next series of motivational quotations prompts managers and employees to create a better workplace and a better organization.

No company can afford not to move forward. It may be at the top of the heap today but at the bottom of the heap tomorrow, if it doesn't.
—James Cash Penney, Founder, JC Penny

If an organization is not moving forward and stays in the comfort of the "status quo," it is headed to the bottom of the heap, the door to extinction. How do companies avoid stagnation that will eventually put them on the bottom of the heap?

The first sentence in a BizShifts-Trends article reads:

Companies must learn to celebrate and support people within the organization who are willing to challenge the status quo, to bring totally different perspectives on delivering value to customers, and to take experimental risks to explore new business models. ("Organizations Are Not Eternal—They Fail: In Fact Some Organizations Are Not Built to Succeed...Seeds of Success and Why Companies Fail," 2012)

One of the first ways to avoid stagnation is to hire employees who think differently than you. If you hire employees who think the same as you and do not provide any new thoughts or ideas to benefit the department, then stagnation is all but guaranteed. When I train on diversity and inclusion and I lead the discussion on recruiting employees, I always ask the training participants, "What do you look for when interviewing new employees?" The two most common responses are qualified applicants, and someone who will "fit in" to the department. When we talk about fitting in the department, the discussion turns to the fact that managers don't have time to supervise a group that is not working together. Many managers feel their job would be easier if they didn't have to manage employees. (Then why are they managers?)

Once managers put the comfort of the department before new ideas and innovative collaboration, stagnation has begun to set in. But the failure to hire innovative employees is not the only reason companies fail.

The same BizShifts-Trends article talks about the other reasons why this happens:
> There are many reasons why companies fail or stagnate, but four reasons continue to come up in almost all cases.
> - *No vision, strategy, or strategic business plan*
> - *Weak or ineffective management*
> - *Lack of information and control systems*
> - *Under capitalization*

What do these four bullet points have to do with evolution? Let's look at them another way:
- Failing to prepare for evolution
- Failing to manage the evolutionary process
- Failing to research the best ways to evolve and control the evolutionary process
- Failing to secure the resources to evolve

The wording is different, but the four points directly address why companies fail or stagnate. Failing to evolve in anyone of those four categories has the same effect: stagnation or extinction.

WORDS OF MOTIVATION FOR EVOLUTION

Whenever I consult or train, there are always managers who do not feel they have any internally generated problems. After I ask a series of questions based on discussions with other managers or in-depth research prior to our conversation, many internal problems find bubble up to the surface. Even after the problem is identified, the manager usually feels that the problem is not big enough to address or it is "contained." This creates an opportunity for further discussion based on two factors: risk and accountability. Internally generated problems are the final component in the analysis of the Biz-Shifts Trends article.

According to statistics from the Association of Insolvency and Restructuring Advisors (AIRA), the majority of business failures (67%) are caused by internally generated problems within the control of management, not by bad luck or external events like an economic recession. Being accountable is a crucial step to overcoming the obstacles that face management. Without someone taking ownership of a problem, nothing changes. Waiting for an external factor, outside of your control, in order to have a reason to change is a sure-fire recipe for business change.

Management accountability has been a frequent and important concept in this book. This BizShifts-Trends article does not specifically address diversity and inclusion, but management accountability crosses all areas of responsibility, including diversity and inclusion. This article links problems within the control of management to a 67% business failure rate. A 67% failure rate is a powerfully motivating figure to make sure managers are accountable for their actions and to minimize their bad actions by removing them from their positions or the organization if necessary. Selfish and contentious managers can lead the organization down to the bottom of the heap, the doorway to extinction.

Where we all think alike, no one thinks very much.
—Walter Lippmann, American writer, reporter, and political commentator

This quote takes us back to the extinction of Nokia mentioned in the first chapter. If all employees think alike, evolution cannot take place. When hiring managers only hire employees who look and think like them,

DIVERSIFY OR DIE: DIVERSITY. INCLUSION. EVOLUTION. SUCCESS.

the hiring manager is limiting the access to the pool of ideas to improve their department. Hiring "yes men" or "yes women" only results in hiring people who will keep the department from moving forward. Evolution only occurs when someone dares to think "outside of the box," or they take the experience from their own background and culture and apply it to an entirely different area.

Imagine a world where Charles Darwin did not think differently and refine the theory of evolution. Imagine a world where Alan Turing did not theorize computer science and artificial intelligence, which led to the personal computer. Imagine a world where Otis Boykin did not invent more than twenty-five electronic devices, including the improved electrical resistor and the control unit for the pacemaker. Imagine a world where Stephanie Kwolek did not invent an unusually light weight and durable fiber that was later used for Kevlar, fiber optic cables, and building materials. Imagine a world where Roberto Landell de Moura did not invent the first wireless telephone. Imagine a world where T. David Petite did not invent Smart Meter technology and patent more than thirty inventions related to networking, remote control activation, and wireless enabled devices.

Now imagine a world where these brilliant and diverse trailblazers were not hired based on their diversity. This happens everyday.

Workplace bullying—in any form—is bad for business. It destroys teamwork, commitment, and morale.
—Tony Morgan, Author

This quote directly links the workplace environment to organizational success. This quote is not saying employees who do not support diversity and inclusion are workplace bullies, but it does show how the abuse of power and the organizational failure to resolve bullying issues can hurt operations. After all, if teamwork is destroyed, how can an organization function?

This quote directly ties into the Darwin quote for this chapter. As selfish and contentious people will not "cohere" and coherence is required for teamwork, selfish and contentious people are bad for business. But there are times when selfish and contentious people take their words and actions too far and create a hostile workplace environment through workplace bullying.

True to the meaning of this motivational quote on workplace bullying, I have managed and conducted hundreds of workplace harassment and workplace bullying investigations and mediations. The harassment and bullying were always very disruptive and costly to the organization. There were never any winners, only different levels of losers.

Workplace bullying has been recognized as an epidemic in the workplace. According to "The Silent Epidemic: Workplace Bullying," a 2011 article in *Psychology Today*:

> *Bullies create a terrible toll within an organization. Their behavior leads to increased level of stress among employees, higher rates of absenteeism, and higher than normal attrition. Because bullies often get results by getting more short-term production out of employees, they are tolerated. One study by John Medina showed that workers stressed by bullying performed 50% worse on cognitive tests. Other studies estimate the financial costs of bullying at $200 billion.*

Since most workplace bullying is not reported or the employee chooses to leave the workplace rather than file a complaint or sue the company, the $200 billion figure is probably much higher. According to an article in *Investopia*, "Financial Impacts of Workplace Bullying," research estimates that 25% – 50% of the workforce has been a victim of some kind of workplace bullying. The article also addresses the financial impact of workplace bullying.

> *Although it may be difficult to tabulate the exact costs that an employer faces when a bully is operating within the organization, there is little doubt there are financial impacts. Despite this dismal fact, some researchers suggest that workplace bullying may be on the rise. There's little doubt that happy employees invest more in the success of the organizations that employ them, so wise employers will take heed and do what they can to increase productivity, employee retention, and morale through taking a hard stance on the issue of workplace bullying.*

DIVERSIFY OR DIE: DIVERSITY. INCLUSION. EVOLUTION. SUCCESS.

These articles directly link workplace bullying to employee morale and the bottom line. After all, as discussed in detail in the next motivational quote, happy employees are good for profits.

Happy employees lead to happy customers, which leads to more profits.
—Vaughn Aust, EVP of Integrated Solutions

Of course an organization with workplace bullying does not have happy employees. If the employees are not happy, their unhappiness may show up in their sales and customer service. Customer service that is less than standard may result in a loss of business. But there are many reasons other than workplace bullying that lead to unhappy employees.

Employee happiness in an organization is heavily based on their relationship with their immediate supervisor. As Darwin says, *"selfish and contentious people will not cohere, and without coherence nothing can be effected."* This means selfish and contentious supervisors will not only result in nothing be effected, but employees will leave the organization. Once the employee leaves, the organization has one less person offering good referrals for the organization's goods and services and as a place of employment.

Good employees quit their manager, not the employer. Some reasons employees quit according to a Forbes article, "Six Reasons Your Best Employees Quit You," are:

1. The organization does not have any vision
2. The employee does not feel a connection to the big picture
3. Supervisors do not feel empathy for their employees
4. The <u>work</u> does not effectively motivate their employees
5. The employee does not feel that they have a career path in the organization
6. Employees do not feel that their work is innovative and fun

Most of these reasons are focused on the employee's concerns that the business or the employee's own career is not evolving. As the employee's supervisor is an important factor in the employee's career, they are also an important reason why employees stay or leave an organization. If employees feel their career is facing extinction in their current position, they will probably leave when another organization gives them an opportunity to evolve.

Employees want to know they are in an organization that is evolving to compete in the marketplace. Employees know organizations that do not evolve will face extinction, and they would rather leave the organization before extinction than face extinction with the organization.

One of the best tools to measure workplace happiness is a workplace climate survey. In my role as a committee member to coordinate climate surveys, I have found that well constructed and coordinated surveys are very instructive in helping the organization evolve. If surveys do not help organizations evolve it is usually not the survey, but the organization's response to the survey answers. Even when employees expressed a clear pattern of concern or unhappiness, if the solution was too complicated or too expensive to resolve, executives either ignored the real cause of the concern or responded with very little resources or effort. This approach only makes matters worse.

At the constitutional level where we work, 90 percent of any decision is emotional. The rational part of us supplies the reasons for supporting our predilections.
—William O. Douglas, Former Associate Justice
of the Supreme Court of the United States

Although this quote is about the decisions Supreme Court justices' make on cases, this quote applies to everyday decisions as well. Everyone uses emotions everyday to make decisions, and then uses logic or rationale to support those decisions.

According to the *BigThink.com* article "Decisions Are Emotional Not Logical: The Neuroscience Behind Decision Making," neuroscientist Antonio Damasio discovered that people with damage in the part of the brain where emotions are generated could not make decisions, even simple ones like what to eat. Based on these findings, Mr. Damasio found that emotions are an important part of our decision-making process.

DIVERSIFY OR DIE: DIVERSITY. INCLUSION. EVOLUTION. SUCCESS.

This is why this chapter is so important to this book. As a leader, you can give your leadership team and supervisors all of the US Census, financial, local and regional demographic data, and marketing data to prove the benefits of diversity and inclusion, and leaders will still make emotional decisions not to support diversity programs. Some employees may even find their own data to support their emotional decision. That is why the start of a diversity and inclusion conversation is to change the hearts, not the minds, of employees who do not support diversity programs.

The best approach is to create a vision for the organization and make all employees part of that vision, especially selfish and contentious employees. The vision should make the employees want to support diversity. How is that accomplished? Appeal to the employee's self-interest. The vision should communicate to the employees why this is good for them and the people around them. In the end, data and figures won't gain their support; creating the vision that it is to their advantage to support diversity and inclusion will.

Diversity: the art of thinking independently together.
—Malcolm Forbes, Publisher, Business Leader, Entrepreneur

A quote about diversity from Malcolm Forbes, an evolutionary leader in publishing and business, is an excellent way to end this chapter. All managers should use this quote to motivate their employees to think "independently together."

This quote takes us back to the Hyundai business example in Chapter 5. Hyundai found a way to use diversity to stop the stale business practice of conventional thinking. Instead, Hyundai used multimedia to encourage employees to think independently together. Once that happened, Hyundai zoomed past the competition.

Use Your Definition of Diversity to Motivate Your Employees

These motivational quotes—used together or separately—could be valuable tools in advancing diversity programs. When faced with a large employee morale problem, use all of the previous motivational quotes. Leaders should recognize the problem, not avoid the problem, and then solve the problem. It is important to realize solving the problem will take time. Once the company is moving forward and the diversity efforts are taking hold, the work environment should experience an increase in morale and employee satisfaction. If happy employees lead to happy customers, who lead to more profits, diversity may be the factor to start or speed up that profitable chain reaction.

Although these quotes are powerful, the best message is the message created by the leadership of the organization. These messages can serve to unify the employees under one common goal or objective. Unifying messages are very motivational and powerful. Whenever a group of people can unify behind one message, the power of the message and power of the people expands exponentially.

The diversity equation and definition of diversity can serve as one of those unifying motivational messages.

Cultural identities + substantial relevance to the organization + impact on organizational effectiveness = definition of diversity.

When using the diversity equation to create the organizational definition of diversity, consider motivation in the "impact on organizational effectiveness." As the definition of diversity will be on the organization's website, social media, ERG information, annual report, marketing materials, and other forms of communication, it can serve as a constant form of motivation. Consistent messages lead to consistent results.

CHAPTER 11
DIVERSIFY AND THRIVE

"But probably the most important point of all is, that the animal or plant should be so highly useful to man, or so much valued by him, that the closest attention should be paid to even the slightest deviation in the qualities or structure of each individual. Unless such attention be paid, nothing can be effected."

— Charles Darwin, *On The Origin of Species*

A common theme of this book has been the diversity equation and the definition of diversity. Both are powerful evolutionary tools. Like most tools, they must be used in an effective manner. The bottom line is in every organization; each individual is the source of evolution. As Darwin says, "the closest attention should be paid to even the slightest deviation in the qualities or structure of each individual. Unless such attention be paid, [to each individual,] nothing can be effected." This chapter focuses on the individual and the next steps in evolution for an organization.

Why Should I Care About Diversity and Inclusion? Revisited

Chapter 1 presented the question, "why should I care about diversity and inclusion?" In this closing chapter, the question has evolved to a statement because the content of the book told you why organizations should care. Evolution includes enjoying pleasure and avoiding pain.

Good News

This book has showcased many diversity challenges, but there is good news. If you reached this portion of the book, at least three things have happened.

DIVERSIFY AND THRIVE

First, you have been exposed to the concepts and recommendations. Second, if you took away at least three new concepts and recommendations from this book, you have started down the path of evolution. If you began to envision new ways to use at least three concepts to improve diversity in your organization, you have personally and professionally evolved in your diversity journey.

These three actions are seeds of evolution. Once these actions take place, diversity has started to create a place for itself to thrive. But these diversity actions need structure, and this comes from the diversity equation and definition of diversity.

The Diversity Equation and the Definition of Diversity

Think of the diversity equation as a "roadmap" and the definition of diversity and inclusion as the first part of the diversity journey. Creating the diversity equation should be a team exercise with employees from all levels of the organization. Limiting the diversity equation team to executives will weaken the effectiveness of diversity and inclusion, as all levels of employees should provide input. One way to engage all employees is to seek input from the Employee Resource Committees (ERCs).

Once the components for the diversity equation have been completed, the next step is to plug the components of the diversity equation into the definition of diversity.

The definition is designed to provide a high-level vision to everyone in the organization, so it should be brief and only contain relevant information. All of the possible options to define each section of the diversity equation cannot be included in the definition of diversity and inclusion. There are other places in the organization where the unused options from the diversity equation can be put to good use:
- Diversity department projects
- Organizational policies
- Employee Resource Committee (ERC) mission statement or projects
- Diversity Council mission statements or projects
- Specific operational diversity programs
- Diversity training programs
- Diversity metrics

DIVERSIFY OR DIE: DIVERSITY. INCLUSION. EVOLUTION. SUCCESS.

Create the measurements to determine the effectiveness of the definition of diversity and inclusion based on the analysis of the diversity equation.

The diversity efforts following the completion of the diversity equation and the definition of diversity and inclusion must be measured to determine effectiveness. Measurements are so important that they are the final component of the diversity equation: "impact on organizational effectiveness." Measurements capturing existing diversity actions provide a way to determine success. Once both metrics have been recorded, the data can be used to improve diversity efforts, which will ensure the diversity efforts are constantly evolving.

The Next Steps in Evolution
What is next step for diversity and inclusion in your organization? That is the ten million dollar question.

Regardless of industry, public or private sector, small business, not for profit, or government agency, the best way to create an effective diversity department starts with these questions:

1. Have you directly linked diversity to your organization's mission and objectives?
2. Have you used the diversity equation to create a definition of diversity?
3. Are the CEO and senior executives actively engaging in the diversity efforts?
4. Are middle managers actively engaging in diversity efforts?
5. Have all leaders been trained in diversity specifically designed for your organization based on your definition of diversity?
6. Have you established reasonable and measurable goals and expectations for the diversity department?
7. Have you established reasonable and measurable goals and expectations for middle management?
8. Have you held managers accountable then failed to meet the measurable diversity goals as they would be held accountable if they failed to meet any other organizational goal?

9. Have you invested significant time, money, and resources to linking diversity to your bottom line?
10. Have you analyzed your current and potential consumer base to determine effective ways to market, sell and provide customer support based on your products and services?

Until these core questions can be answered with measurable solutions, an organization does not have the information or resources to use diversity to evolve.

In the end, evolution will happen; the question is, on what side of evolution will your organization stand? As diversity is a key component of evolution, you can diversify or die, or you can diversify and thrive!

AFTERWORD

Congratulations on completing *Diversify or Die*. Diversity and inclusion is a challenging and controversial topic, but when utilized correctly, everyone benefits. Once the power and emotional challenges are set aside, real diversity and inclusion work can take place to benefit the organization.

Now the question is, "what are you going to do with the information you learned?"

Diversify or Die is not designed to make you an expert in diversity and inclusion, but it is designed to give you tools to manage your personal diversity journey to benefit you and your organization. Your personal diversity journey may include managing a team, committee, department, or an entire organization. The "Evolve and Succeed" section at the end of the chapters provide steps to use diversity and inclusion in your workday. These steps will start your diversity journey, but diversity is a "team sport" not an "individual sport." Diversity and inclusion requires interactions with team members, co-workers, and friends. But diversity also requires structure at an organizational level; this is where we can work together to evolve your organization.

AFTERWORD

As stated in *Diversify or Die*, diversity and inclusion consulting and training should be highly specialized and customized for every organization. All of my trainings are designed for my clients' specific issues and culture. Even if you have a diversity program or department, have your diversity efforts evolved with your organization? Or from a different viewpoint, is your organization stagnant and in need of evolutionary diversity thinking? I look forward to helping you answer these questions and many more.

I hope *Diversify or Die* makes you ask the question, "are we evolving or are we facing extinction?" If you start asking that question, the book has met one of its major objectives. I ask myself that question all of the time since I started writing this book. I am not only the author of *Diversify or Die;* I am also a client.

Thank you for sharing this diversity and inclusion journey with me. I look forward to sharing many more journeys with all of you.

Eric L. Guthrie, Esq. CDE

BIBLIOGRAPHY

Abbott. "An Inclusive Culture." *Abbott* (2015) http://www.abbott.com/careers/diversity-and-inclusion.html.

———. "Who We Are." *Abbott* (2015) http://www.abbott.com/about-abbott/who-we-are.html.

ABC 7 News. "GEICO to Pay $6 Million Dollar Settlement for Overcharging Poor." ABC 7 News (2015). http://abc7news.com/automotive/geico-to-pay-$6-million-settlement-for-over-charging-poor/955915/.

Alexander, Donnell. "Racism Literally Costs America $2 Trillion... Ready to Stop Payment?" *Take Part*, December 13, 2013. http://www.takepart.com/article/2013/12/13/racism-literally-costs-america-too-much-continue.com/end.

Alter, Charlotte. "How Sandra Day O'Conner Became the First Woman Supreme Court Justice." *Time,* July 7, 2016. http://time.com/4380619/sandra-day-oconnor-35-years/.

American Alliance of Museums. "Diversity and Inclusion Policy." American Alliance of Museums. http://www.aam-us.org/about-us/strategic-plan/diversity-and-inclusion-policy. (Accessed August 29, 2016)

Badger, Emily. "What Happened to the Millions of Workers Granted Legal Status Under Ronald Regan?" *The Washington Post,* November 26, 2014, https://www.washingtonpost.com/news/wonk/wp/2014/11/26/what-happened-to-the-millions-of-immigrants-granted-legal-status-under-ronald-reagan/.

Ball, Molly. "How Gay Marriage Became a Constitutional Right." *The Atlantic,* July 1, 2015. http://www.theatlantic.com/politics/archive/2015/07/gay-marriage-supreme-court-politics-activism/397052/.

BIBLIOGRAPHY

Bio. "5 Female Inventors that Changed Life as We Know It." *Bio* (2015). http://www.biography.com/news/famous-women-inventors-biography.

Birkinshaw, Julian. "Why Corporate Giants Fail to Change." *Fortune,* May 8, 2013. http://fortune.com/2013/05/08/why-corporate-giants-fail-to-change/.

"Black Chairman and CEO's of Fortune 500 Companies." *Black Entrepreneurs and Executives,* January 29, 2015. https://www.blackentrepreneurprofile.com/fortune-500-ceos/

Bregman, Peter. "Diversity Training Doesn't Work." *Harvard Business Review* (2012).

Bruner, Diane. "Equal Educational Nights Act (EEOA)." *Law and Higher Education* (2015). http://lawhigheredu.com/52-equal-educational-opportunities-act-eeoa.html.

Brunner, Borgna and Beth Rowen. *"Timeline of Affirmative Milestones."* Fact Monster (2016). http://www.infoplease.com/spot/affirmativetimeline1.html.

BusinessDictionary.com, s.v. "Diversity," *BusinessDictionary.com* http://www.businessdictionary.com/definition/diversity.html. (Accessed August 23, 2016)

Camp, Jim. "Decisions are Emotional not Logical: The Neuroscience Behind Decision Making." *Big Think.* http://bigthink.com/experts-corner/decisions-are-emotional-not-logical-the-neuroscience-behind-decision-making. (Accessed August 23, 2016)

CB Insights Research. "Venture Capital Demographics – 87% of all VC Backed Founders are White; All Asian Teams Raise Largest Funding Rounds." *CB Insights* (2010). https://www.cbinsights.com/blog/venture-capital-demographics-87-percent-vc-backed-founders-white-asian-teams-raise-largest-funding/

Chan, Sewell. "Revisiting 1969 and the Start of Gay Liberation." *New York Times,* June 8, 2009. http://cityroom.blogs.nytimes.com/2009/06/08/nypl-stonewall-post/?_r=0.

Chief Editor. "Famous Hispanic Inventors." *NLCATP* (blog), March 9, 2014. http://nlcatp.org/famous-hispanic-inventors/.

Clemetson, Lynette. "Hispanics now Largest Minority Census Shows." *New York Times,* January 22, 2003. http://www.nytimes.com/2003/01/22/us/hispanics-now-largest-minority-census-shows.html.

The Coca Cola Company. "Form 10K." *The Coca Cola Company* (2015). https://www.coca-colacompany.com/content/dam/journey/us/en/private/fileassets/pdf/2015/02/2014-annual-report-on-form-10-k.pdf.

———. "Global Diversity Mission." *The Coca Cola Company.* http://www.coca-colacompany.com/our-company/diversity/global-diversity-mission. (Accessed August 25, 2016)

Cohn, Emily. "CVS Caught Illegally Charging Women for Birth Control." *Huffington Post,* September 24, 2014. http://www.huffingtonpost.com/2014/09/24/cvs-birth-control-charge-illegal_n_5875174.html.

Colgate-Palmolive. "Colgate-Palmolive 2014 Annual Report." (2015) http://www.colgate.com/us/en/annual-reports/2014/common/pdf/Colgate%202014%20AR%20Web%20Ready.pdf.

Consumer Financial Protection Bureau. "CFPB and DOJ Order Ally to Pay $80 Million to Consumers Harmed by Discriminatory Auto Loan Pricing." (2013) http://www.consumerfinance.gov/about-us/newsroom/cfpb-and-doj-order-ally-to-pay-80-million-to-consumers-harmed-by-discriminatory-auto-loan-pricing/.

BIBLIOGRAPHY

Darwin, Charles. *The Descent of Man and Selection in Relation to Sex.* London: John Murray, 1871.

———. On The Origin of Species by the Means of Natural Selection. London: John Murray, 1859.

Dimarco, Chris. "Top Ten Most Expensive Law Suits of 2013." *Inside Counsel* (2014). http://www.insidecounsel.com/2014/07/08/top-10-most-expensive-discrimination-settlements-o?slreturn=1464619514&page=4.

DiversityInc. "DiversityInc Top 50 Lists Since 2001." *DiversityInc.* http://www.diversityinc.com/all-diversityinc-top-50-lists/. (Accessed August 23, 2016)

Donn, Jeff. "After a Century of Overcharging Blacks, Insurance Companies are Facing Suits." *USA Today,* October 10, 2004. http://usatoday30.usatoday.com/money/industries/insurance/2004-10-10-insurance-suits_x.htm.

Efron, Lewis. "Six Reasons Your Best Employees Quit You." *Forbes,* June 24, 2013. http://www.forbes.com/sites/louisefron/2013/06/24/six-reasons-your-best-employees-quit-you/#3c7b67c820a1.

Elias, Jennifer. "Venture Capital in Silicon Valley Isn't Diverse, and That's a Problem for America." *Fast Company,* March 4, 2015. https://www.fastcompany.com/3042887/diversity-in-tech-follow-the-money-vcs.

Eng, Dinah. "Bob Johnson Moves Way Beyond BET." *Fortune,* November 7, 2012. http://fortune.com/2012/11/07/bob-johnson-moves-way-beyond-bet/.

Exhibits. "Martin Luther King Jr. and the 'I have a Dream Speech.'" National Archives. https://www.archives.gov/nyc/exhibit/mlk.html. (Accessed August 22, 2016)

Espinoza, Lucas E. and Luis. E. Espinoza. "Hernandez v. Texas: The Fight for Mexican American Rights." Essay, Texas Woman's University, 2005. http://www.twu.edu/downloads/history-government/Espinoza_Revised_Ibid_Essay_16.pdf.

Fowler, Janet. "Financial Impacts of Workplace Bullying." *Investopedia* (2016). http://www.investopedia.com/financial-edge/0712/financial-impacts-of-workplace-bullying.aspx.

Gajilan, Arlin T., and Earl G. Graves. "Earl Graves Black Enterprise." *CNN Money,* September 1, 2003. http://money.cnn.com/magazines/fsb/fsb_archive/2003/09/01/350792/.

The Gale Group, Inc. "Immigration Laws and Policies Since the 1980s." *Encylopedia.com.* http://www.encyclopedia.com/topic/Immigration_and_Nationality_Act_of_1952.aspx. (Accessed August 23, 2016)

Giang, Vivian. "The Growing Business of Detecting Unconscious Bias." *Fast Company,* May 5, 2015. http://www.fastcompany.com/3045899/hit-the-ground-running/the-growing-business-of-detecting-unconscious-bias.

The George Washington University. "Diversity and Inclusion Defined." The George Washington University. https://diversity.gwu.edu/diversity-and-inclusion-defined. (Accessed August 29, 2016)

Gino, Francesca. "What Facebook's Anti-Bias Training Get's Right." *Harvard Business Review,* August 2015. https://hbr.org/2015/08/what-facebooks-anti-bias-training-program-gets-right.

Glass, Andrew. "Congress Passes Civil Rights Act Aug. 29, 1957." *Politico,* August 2007. http://www.politico.com/story/2007/08/congress-passes-civil-rights-act-aug-29-1957-005470.

BIBLIOGRAPHY

Greenhouse, Linda. "High Court Widens Workplace Claims on Sex Harassment." *The New York Times,* March 5, 1998. http://www.nytimes.com/1998/03/05/us/high-court-widens-workplace-claims-in-sex-harassment.html?pagewanted=all.

Guzman, René A. "Spanish Language TV Born in S.A." *San Antonio Express-News,* June 21, 2015. http://www.expressnews.com/150years/culture/article/San-Antonio-is-home-to-the-nation-s-first-6340586.php.

Handfield, Ron, PhD. "A Brief History of Outsourcing." *NC State Poole College of Management Supply Chain Resource Cooperative* (2006). https://scm.ncsu.edu/scm-articles/article/a-brief-history-of-outsourcing.

Hendricks, Drew. "Complete History of Social Media: Then and Now." *Small Business Trends,* May 8, 2013. http://smallbiztrends.com/2013/05/the-complete-history-of-social-media-infographic.html.

Hess, Alexander E.M., and Thomas C. Frochlich. "The 10 Dying U.S. Industries." *USA Today,* December 23, 2014. http://www.usatoday.com/story/money/business/2014/12/23/247-wall-st-dying-thriving-industries/20185247/.

HG.org. "What is Affirmative Action and Why Was it Created?" *HG.org.* n.d. https://www.hg.org/article.asp?id=31524. (Accessed August 23, 2016)

Hill, Napoleon. *Think and Grow Rich.* New York: The Ralston Society, 1938.

HR Hot Topics. "Age Discrimination in Employment Act." *HR Hero.* n.d. http://topics.hrhero.com/age-discrimination-in-employment-act-adea/#.

Humphreys, Jeffrey M. "The Multicultural Economy." *Georgia Business and Economic Conditions no.* 67-3 (2007). https://www.terry.uga.edu/media/documents/gbec/GBEC0703Q.pdf.

International Business Machines. "2014 IBM Annual Report." *International Business Machines* (2015). https://www.ibm.com/annualreport/2014/bin/assets/IBM-Annual-Report-2014.pdf.

———. "Diversity and Inclusion." *International Business Machines.* http://www-03.ibm.com/employment/us/diverse/. (Accessed August 24, 2016)

Innovate Product Design. "Famous LGBT Inventors and Their Inventions." *Innovate Product Design.* June 13, 2016. http://www.innovate-design.com/famous-lgbt-inventors-inventions/.

Internet Society. "A Brief History of the Internet and Related Works." *Internet Society,* n.d. http://www.internetsociety.org/internet/what-internet/history-internet/brief-history-internet-related-networks. (Accessed August 22, 2016)

Johnston, William, and Arnold Packer. *Workforce 2000: Work and Workers for the 21st Century.* Indianapolis: Hudson Institute, 1987.

Judy, Richard, and Carol D'Amico. *Workforce 2020: Work and Workers for the 21st Century* Indianapolis: Hudson Institute, 1997.

Krogstad, Jens Manuel. "Social Media Preferences Vary by Race and Ethnicity." *Fact Tank,* Pew Research Center, February 3, 2015. http://www.pewresearch.org/fact-tank/2015/02/03/social-media-preferences-vary-by-race-and-ethnicity/.

Kurland, Robyn, and Corrine Yu. "First Hispanic Justice Confirmed to the U.S. Supreme Court." *Civil Rights Monitor,* Winter 2016. http://www.civilrights.org/monitor/winter-2010/first-hispanic-justice-2009.html.

BIBLIOGRAPHY

Labaton, Stephen. "Denny's Restaurants to Pay $54 Million in Race Bias Suits." *New York Times,* May 25, 1994. http://www.nytimes.com/1994/05/25/us/denny-s-restaurants-to-pay-54-million-in-race-bias-suits.html?pagewanted=all.

The Learning Network. "May 17, 1954: Supreme Court Declares School Segregation Unconstitutional in Brown v. Board." *The Learning Network (blog).* May 17, 2012. http://learning.blogs.nytimes.com/2012/05/17/may-17-1954-supreme-court-declares-school-segregation-unconstitutional-in-brown-v-board-of-education/?_r=0.

Levine, Sheen, and Evan Apfelbaum, et al. "Ethnic Diversity Deflates Price Bubbles." *Proceedings of the National Academy of Sciences of the United States of America.* (2014)

Listverse Staff. "Top 10 African American Inventors." *Listverse,* October 29, 2007. http://listverse.com/2007/10/29/top-10-african-american-inventors/.

MacMillian, Ian, and Rita MacGrath. "Discovering New Points of Differentiation." *The Harvard Business Review,* July 1997. https://hbr.org/1997/07/discovering-new-points-of-differentiation.

Mann, Joseph, and Maggie Morales. "NBC Buys Telemundo in 2.7 Billion Dollar Deal." *Sun Sentinel,* October 12, 2001. http://articles.sun-sentinel.com/2001-10-12/news/0110120258_1_telemundo-debt-hialeah-based-telemundo-communications-hispanic.

Marriott International. "Marriott 2014 Annual Report." *Marriott International* (2015). http://investor.shareholder.com/mar/marriottAR14/index.html.

———. "2014 Report on Global Diversity and Inclusion." *Marriott International.* http://www.marriott.com/Multimedia/PDF/Corp

orateResponsibility/2014SustainMicroRpt_GloDivers_hr.pdf. (Accessed August 24, 2016)

Mauboussin, Michael. "The True Measure of Success." *Harvard Business Review* (2012).

McAuliff, Michael, and Casey Smith, et al. "Barack Obama Becomes The First African American to be Nominated by a Major Political Party in 2008." *New York Daily News* August 27, 2015. http://www.nydailynews.com/news/politics/obama-nominated-president-2009-article-1.2338931

McBride, Alex. "Regents of University of California." *The Supreme Court* (2007). http://www.pbs.org/wnet/supremecourt/rights/landmark_regents.html.

McDonald, Kelly. *Crafting the Customer Service Experience for People Not Like You: How to Delight and Engage the Customers You Don't Understand.* Hoboken: John Wiley and Sons, Inc., 2012.

McQueen, Lee. "John Harold Johnson." *Encylopedia.com* (2005). http://www.encyclopedia.com/topic/John_Harold_Johnson.aspx.

Merck & Co., Inc. "Form 10-K." *Merck & Co., Inc.* (2015). http://s21.q4cdn.com/755037021/files/doc_financials/annualReports/2015/MRK_2015_Form_10-K_FINAL_r879.pdf.

———. "Employee Diversity." *Merck & Co. Inc.* http://www.merck.com/about/how-we-operate/diversity/employee-diversity.html. (Accessed August 25, 2016)

Minority Business Development Agency. "Who We Are." *Minority Business Development Agency* (2016). http://www.mbda.gov/main/who-mbda/about-minority-business-development-agency.

Mitchell, Allison. "To Understand Clinton's Moment, Consider that it Came 32 Years After Ferraro's." *New York Times,* June 12, 2016. http://www.nytimes.com/2016/06/12/us/politics/women-white-house-clinton-geraldine-ferraro.html.

BIBLIOGRAPHY

Molina, Brett. "Apple CEO Tim Cook: 'I'm Proud to be Gay.'" *USA Today,* October 30, 2014. http://www.usatoday.com/story/tech/2014/10/30/tim-cook-comes-out/18165361/.

Mulligan, Thomas, and Chris Kraul. "Texaco Settles Bias Suit for $176 Million." *Los Angeles Times,* November 16, 1996. http://articles.latimes.com/1996-11-16/news/mn-65290_1_texaco-settles-race-bias-suit.

Napoli, Philip, and Nancy Gillis. "Media Ownership and the Diversity Index: Outlining a Social Science Research Agenda." *McGannon Center Working Paper Series* (2008).

National Organization of Women. "Who We Are." *National Organization of Women* (2015). http://now.org/about/who-we-are/.

Nieva, Richard. "Ashes to Ashes, Peer to Peer: An Oral History of Napster." *Fortune,* September 5, 2013. http://fortune.com/2013/09/05/ashes-to-ashes-peer-to-peer-an-oral-history-of-napster/.

Nusbaum, Matt, AD. "OFCCP Cleans House." *Lexology* (2013). http://www.lexology.com/library/detail.aspx?g=9388db4b-0781-44c4-8cae-6bbec24c3310.

"Oprah Winfrey's Official Biography." *Oprah,* n.d. http://www.oprah.com/pressroom/Oprah-Winfreys-Official-Biography (Accessed August 23, 2016)

Pacer Center. "ADA Q&A: The Rehabilitation Act and ADA Connection." *Pacer Center* (2016). http://www.pacer.org/publications/adaqa/adaqa.asp.

Pelofsky, Jeremy, and James Vicini. "BofA's Countrywide to Pay $335 Million Over Bias Case." *Reuters* (2011). http://www.reuters.com/article/us-boa-countrywide-idUSTRE7BK1UW20111222.

Perry, Mark. "Fortune 500 firms in 1955 vs. 2014; 89% are Gone, and We're all Better off Because of that Dynamic 'Creative Destruction.'" *AEI* August 18, 2014. https://www.aei.org/publication/fortune-500-firms-in-1955-vs-2014-89-are-gone-and-were-all-better-off-because-of-that-dynamic-creative-destruction/.

Prochilo, Dan. "Chicago to Pay $2M to Settle Firefighter Applicant's Bias Suit." *Law 360* (2013). http://www.law360.com/articles/439904/chicago-to-pay-2m-to-settle-firefighter-applicants-bias-suit.

Proctor and Gamble. "P&G 2014 Annual Report." *Proctor and Gamble* (2014). http://www.pginvestor.com/interactive/lookandfeel/4004124/PG_Annual_Report_2014.pdf.

———. "Diversity and Inclusion." *Proctor and Gamble.* http://us.pg.com/who-we-are/our-approach/diversity-inclusion. (Accessed August 24, 2016)

Pro Publica, Inc. "Bailout Recipients." *Propublica,* August 4, 2016. https://projects.propublica.org/bailout/list.

Prudential Financial, Inc. "PRU 2014 Prudential Financial Annual Report." Prudential Financial, Inc. https://www.prudential.com/documents/public/Prudential-AR2014.pdf. (Accessed August 12, 2015)

Radicals & Visionaries. "John H. Johnson: The Voice of Black America." *Entrepreneur,* October 10, 2008. https://www.entrepreneur.com/article/197650.

Ramsey, Mike, and Evan Ramstad. "Once a Global Also-Ran, Hyundai Zooms Forward." *Wall Street Journal,* June 30, 2011.

Richwine, Lisa, and David Adams. "New U.S. TV News Network Fuses News, Satire for Young Hispanics." *Reuters* (2013). http://www.reuters.com/article/us-media-fusion-idUSBRE99Q04C20131027

BIBLIOGRAPHY

Roosevelt, Franklin D. "Order 8802." Equal Employment Opportunity Commission (1941). https://www.eeoc.gov/eeoc/history/35th/thelaw/eo-8802.html.

Roosevelt Thomas Consulting and Training. "Definitions of Diversity." Roosevelt Thomas Consulting and Training. http://www.rthomas-consulting.com/#/definitions-of-diversity/4539543895. (Accessed August 29, 2016)

Santoli, Michael. "The Stock Market is Shrinking Despite Record High Indexes." *Yahoo Finance* (2013). http://finance.yahoo.com/blogs/michael-santoli/the-stock-market-is--shrinking---despite-record-high-indexes-171141756.html.

SHRM. "Definition of Diversity" *SHRM* (2008). https://webcache.googleusercontent.com/search?q=cache:bjswagSNefAJ:https://community.shrm.org/HigherLogic/System/DownloadDocumentFile.ashx%3FDocumentFileKey%3D1142a81c-e083-6091-7edb-e15725c401d6+&cd=1&hl=en&ct=clnk&gl=us&client=safari.

Thomas, Roosevelt R. *Beyond Race and Gender: Unleashing the Power of Your Total Workforce by Managing Diversity.* New York: American Management Association, 1991.

Tumbleweed Connection. "Worst to First: Denny's Restaurant Chain Buries Racist Image." *Free Republic* (2002). http://www.freerepublic.com/focus/f-news/660324/posts.

Turner, Ani. "The Business Case for Racial Equality." *Altarum Institute* (2013). http://altarum.org/sites/default/files/uploaded-publication-files/WKKF%20Business%20Case%20for%20Racial%20Equity.pdf.

United States Census Bureau. "2010 Census Data." *US Census Bureau 2010.* http://www.census.gov/2010census/data/. (Accessed August 22, 2016)

United States Department of Labor. "History of Executive Order 11246." US Department of Labor. https://www.dol.gov/ofccp/about/50thAnniversaryHistory.html. (Accessed August 20, 2016)

———. "OFCCP 50th Anniversary Timeline." US Department of Labor. https://www.dol.gov/featured/ofccp50/alternate.version.timeline.htm.

United Way. "Diversity and Inclusion." *United Way,* n.d. http://www.unitedway.org/about/diversity-and-inclusion. (Accessed August 22, 2016)

US Census Bureau. "U.S. Census Bureau Survey of Business Owners Preliminary Estimates of Business Ownership by Gender, Ethnicity, Race, and Veteran Status: 2007 Census Bureau." *US Census Bureau* (2015). http://documentslide.com/documents/us-census-bureau-survey-of-business-owners-preliminary-estimates-of-business.html.

US Department of Commerce, Minority Business Development Agency. "The Emerging Marketplace, Minority Purchasing Power: 2000 – 2045." MBDA (2000). http://www.ethniccapital.com/uploads/1/2/2/9/12297431/buying_power_methodology_mbda.pdf.

———. "Highlights." MBDA. http://www.mbda.gov/main/mbda-history. (Accessed August 20, 2016)

US Department of Education. "Title IX and Sex Education." *US Department of Education* (2015). http://www2.ed.gov/about/offices/list/ocr/docs/tix_dis.html.

US Equal Employment Opportunity Commission. "Charge Statistics FY 1997 Through FY 2015." *US Equal Employment Opportunity Commission.* https://www.eeoc.gov/eeoc/statistics/enforcement/charges.cfm (Accessed August 23, 2016)

Verizon. "Verizon 2014 Annual Report." *Verizon.* https://www.verizon.com/about/sites/default/files/2014_vz_annual_report.pdf.

BIBLIOGRAPHY

———. "Who We Are." *Verizon.* http://www.verizon.com/about/our-company/diversity-inclusion (Accessed August 24, 2016)

Volvo Group Global. "Global KPIs." *Volvo Group Global.* http://www.volvogroup.com/group/global/en-gb/career/life%20at%20volvo%20group/diversity/measures_of_success/pages/global_kpis.aspx. (Accessed August 20, 2016)

Vedantam, Shankar. "Most Diversity Training Ineffective, Study Finds." *The Washington Post,* January 19, 2008. http://www.washingtonpost.com/wp-dyn/content/article/2008/01/19/AR2008011901899.html.

Walker, Blair S., and Reginald Lewis. *Why Should White Guys Have All of the Fun?* Baltimore: Black Classic Press, 2005.

Wells Fargo. "Culture Counts. An Unwavering Focus on the Customer." *Wells Fargo Annual Report 2014* (2015). https://www08.wellsfargomedia.com/assets/pdf/about/investor-relations/annual-reports/2014-annual-report.pdf.

The White House, Office of the Press Secretary. "Executive Order 13583—Establishing a Coordinated Government-wide Initiative to Promote Diversity and Inclusion in the Federal Workforce." *The White House,* News Release, August 18, 2011. https://www.whitehouse.gov/the-press-office/2011/08/18/executive-order-13583-establishing-coordinated-government-wide-initiativ.

White Papers. "Employees that Drive Business," *Jennifer Brown Consulting,* n.d. http://jenniferbrownconsulting.com/cisco-jbc-driving-business-next-practices-for-ergs/. (Accessed August 22, 2016)

Williams, Juan, and Alex Cohen. "Thurgood Marshall's Historic Appointment." *NPR June 13, 2007.* http://www.npr.org/templates/story/story.php?storyId=11012268.

Williams, Ray. "The Silent Epidemic: Workplace Bullying." *Psychology Today,* May 3, 2011. https://www.psychologytoday.com/blog/wired-success/201105/the-silent-epidemic-workplace-bullying.

Wright, Peter, and Stephen Ferris, et al. "Competitiveness Through Management of Diversity: Effects on Stock Price Valuation." *Academy of Management Journal* (1995). http://amj.aom.org/content/38/1/272.short.

Zapotosky, Matt, and Danielle Douglas. "Chevy Chase Bank Accused of Overcharging Minorities; Capital One to Pay $2.85 Million." *The Washington Post,* October 1, 2013. https://www.washingtonpost.com/local/crime/chevy-chase-bank-accused-of-overcharging-minorities-capital-one-agrees-to-pay-285m/2013/10/01/267df08e-2ab4-11e3-97a3-ff2758228523_story.html.

Zeleny, Jeff. "Obama Clinches Nomination; First Black Candidate to Lead a Major Party Ticket." *New York Times,* June 4, 2008. http://www.nytimes.com/2008/06/04/us/politics/04elect.html.

INDEX

A

Abbott Laboratories, 123, 136-137, 139
Affirmative Action, 9, 20-24, 36, 49, 58-59, 62, 64, 73-76, 82, 84, 91, 94, 112, 115, 118, 138, 175
AIG, 104, 106
Annual Reports, 73, 82, 112
Applicants, 10, 11, 108, 138, 144, 168
Asians, 31, 48-52
Augsburger, David, 142
Aust, Vaughn, 148
Automated Teller Machines (ATM)
Avon, 49

B

Baby Boomers, 29, 35, 43
Bank of America, 32, 104
Bankruptcy, 18
Beagle, 14-15
Beatrice International Foods, 46, 57
Billionaire, 47, 53
Black Entertainment Television, 45
Black Wall Street, 42
   Greenwood Neighborhood, 42
   Brown v. Board of Education, 43, 163

C

Center for American Progress, 62
Chesterton, G.K., 135
Chrysler, 104
Citigroup, 104
Class Action Law Suits, 34
Clinton, Hillary
Coca-Cola, 19, 109, 126, 127, 129, 158
Colgate Palmolive, 111, 119, 128-129, 131, 158
Colleges, 35-36, 48, 50, 69
College Administrator, 51, 166
College Professor

C

Colonial BancGroup, 155
Consumer Goods, 108, 111, 120-121, 129, 131, 135
Cook, Tim, 49
Crowdfunding, 56
Cultural Identities, 29, 38, 78, 80, 149
Culture, 4, 6-7, 9, 12, 14-15, 20, 23, 26-27, 29, 34-35, 38-39, 51, 54-55, 57, 63, 76, 78, 83, 86, 88-89, 111-114, 120, 122, 128, 136, 144, 155-156, 161, 169

D

Darwin, Charles, 12-16
Denny's Restaurants, 33, 138-140, 163, 167
Department of Labor, 52
Discrimination, 32-33, 71, 77, 95, 137-138, 159, 161
Diversity
   Councils, 6, 39, 79, 83, 89-92
   Definition, 35, 134
   Department, 8-9, 65, 67-73, 75, 77, 79, 81, 151-152
   Equation, 24, 27, 29-30, 35, 38, 40, 78, 80, 90, 92, 97-98, 100, 132, 134, 152
   Inc., 47, 100, 105-112, 114, 116, 118, 120, 122, 124, 126, 128, 129, 159
   Metrics, 6, 65, 79, 94-95, 97-101, 151
   Practitioner, 24, 70, 90, 99
Douglas, William O., 147

E

Eastman Kodak, 46 51
Employee Resource Groups, 6, 39, 79, 106
Engagement, 9, 28, 61, 92, 101
Equal Employment Opportunity, 9

DIVERSIFY OR DIE: DIVERSITY. INCLUSION. EVOLUTION. SUCCESS.

E

Equal Employment Opportunity Commission, 167-168
Ethnicity, 25-26, 34, 38, 48, 56, 162, 168
Evolution, 1, 9, 13-17, 21-23, 30, 38, 40-43, 49-50, 53-54, 59, 61-67, 71-72, 76-81, 83, 92, 94, 100, 103, 133, 135, 137, 139, 141, 143, 145, 147, 149
Executive Orders, 34, 49
    8802, 43
    10925, 44
    11246, 44
    11375, 44
    13583, 49
Extinction, 1-2, 13, 18-19, 21, 37, 40-41, 63-65, 68, 81, 103-104, 139, 141-143, 147, 155

F

Facebook, 56, 137, 160
Fannie Mae, 104
Ferraro, Geraldine, 46, 164
Forbes, 19, 43, 46, 103, 146, 159
Forbes, Malcolm, 148
Freddie Mac, 104

G

Gay Rights Movement, 45
General Motors, 20, 104
Generation X, 29
Generation Y, 29
GMAC (now Ally Financial), 33, 104
Great Recession, 103, 131
Grutter v. Bollinger, 48
Guaranty Financial Group, 103

H

Hernandez v. Texas, 43, 160
Hill, Napoleon, 139-140, 161
Honda, 34
Hospitality, 112-113
Human Resources, 9-11, 24, 64, 70-71, 83, 90-91, 100

I

Inclusion, 95-96, 110-114, 118
International Business Machines, 109, 120,
Internet 47, 54-55, 57, 110, 162
Inventors, 157-158, 162-163

J

J.P. Morgan Chase, 104
Johnson, Lyndon B., 44

K

Key Performance Indicators, 95
Kennedy, John F., 44

L

Languages, 39, 51
Latinos, 30-31, 34, 34, 53, 56-57
Legal, 11, 18, 24, 34, 42, 49-50, 55, 59-60
Lehman Brothers, 103
LGBT, 9, 29, 35, 75
Lewis, Reginald, 46, 53, 169

M

Marketing, 1, 6-7, 11, 20, 24, 39, 50, 54, 57, 66
Marriott International, 112-113, 163
Marshall, Thurgood, 44, 169
Merck & Co., Inc., 109, 124-125, 164
Mergers and Acquisitions, 43, 50, 53-54
Middle Management, 66-68, 76, 80, 152
Millennials, 29, 35
Minority Business Development Agency, 44, 164
Morehouse College, 2
Morgan, Tony, 144
Mortgage Crisis, 31
Motivation, 134-135, 137, 139, 141, 143, 145, 147, 149

N

National Organization for Women (NOW), 44
Native Americans, 30, 46-50

172

INDEX

N
Natural Selection, 12, 16, 41, 59, 69, 94, 102-104, 159
New York Stock Exchange (NYSE)
Nokia, 2,143
Not for Profit, 17, 35, 38, 55, 152

O
Obama, Barak, 48-49, 164
Obergefell, et al v. Hodges Director, Ohio Department of Health, et al, 49
OFCCP, 105, 165, 168
Oncale v. Sundowner Offshore Systems, 47
Operations, 18, 37, 72, 90, 116, 118, 144
Opportunity 2000 Award
Organizational Effectiveness, 29, 35, 38, 72, 78-82, 97, 149, 152
Out Sourcing

P
Penney, James Cash, 141
Proctor and Gamble, 109, 118-119, 127, 166
Professor, 2, 36
Prudential Financial, 109, 116-117, 166

Q
Qualified, 7, 31-32, 64, 82, 86, 100, 142
Quota, 7, 45, 67, 73, 141

R
Racism, 55, 62, 156
Realtor, 36-37, 136
Retention, 36, 61, 79, 86, 92, 96-97, 100
Robbins, Anthony, 137

S
Sales, 1, 5, 7, 11, 20, 23-24, 27, 39, 46, 50, 53-54, 72-73, 86-89, 92, 95, 107, 114, 133
Small Business, 11, 17, 19, 36-37, 56, 152, 161
Social Media, 6, 23, 50, 54-58, 89, 149, 161-162

S
Society for Human Resource Management (SHRM), 25, 27
Sotamayor, Sonia
Stock Exchange, 105, 107, 110, 112, 114, 116, 118, 120, 122, 124, 126, 128
Stock Market, 11,19,102-105,107-109, 111, 113, 115, 117, 119, 121, 123, 125, 127, 129, 131, 133-134, 167
Stocks, 19, 100, 102, 105, 107-109, 131-132, 134
Supplier Diversity, 30, 106, 139
Supreme Court, 43-45, 47-50, 147, 162,164
Survival of the Fittest, 12, 15-16

T
Telemundo, 43,47,53,163,
Think Tanks, 85
Thomas, Roosevelt, 26, 28, 47, 61, 167
Timeline, 41-43, 49-50, 53, 134, 157, 168
Title VII, 34, 47
Training, 24, 51-52, 65, 67, 71, 73, 76-79, 81-83, 136-139, 142, 151, 155, 157, 160, 167,169
Tulsa, Oklahoma, 42
Twitter, 56

U
United Way, 26, 28, 168
University of California v. Bakke, 45
Univision, 44, 49, 53

V
Verizon Wireless, 114-115, 168-169
Veterans, 25, 29, 35, 48, 65, 114

W
Wachovia, 111
Washington Mutual, 103
Wells Fargo, 104, 109-111,169

173

CPSIA information can be obtained at www.ICGtesting.com
Printed in the USA
BVOW06*2120080916

461560BV00001B/1/P